Redefining Instructional Leadership

Redefining Instructional Leadership

The Skills and Energy Required of an Instructional Leader

John R. Jones and Misty Henry

ROWMAN & LITTLEFIELD
Lanham • Boulder • New York • London

Published by Rowman & Littlefield
An imprint of The Rowman & Littlefield Publishing Group, Inc.
4501 Forbes Boulevard, Suite 200, Lanham, Maryland 20706
www.rowman.com

86-90 Paul Street, London EC2A 4NE

Copyright © 2022 by John R. Jones and Misty Henry

All rights reserved. No part of this book may be reproduced in any form or by any electronic or mechanical means, including information storage and retrieval systems, without written permission from the publisher, except by a reviewer who may quote passages in a review.

British Library Cataloguing in Publication Information Available

Library of Congress Cataloging-in-Publication Data
Names: Jones, John R., 1949- author. | Henry, Misty, 1982- author.
Title: Redefining instructional leadership : the skills and energy required of an instructional leader / by John R. Jones and Misty Henry.
Description: Lanham, Maryland : Rowman & Littlefield, 2022. | Includes bibliographical references. | Summary: "Redefining Instructional Leadership: The Skills and Energy Required of an Instructional Leader focuses on instructional improvement and how school leaders must function as instructional leaders in order to help teachers improve their overall performance in teaching-because better teacher performance leads to greater student achievement"— Provided by publisher.
Identifiers: LCCN 2022020876 (print) | LCCN 2022020877 (ebook) | ISBN 9781475861310 (cloth) | ISBN 9781475861327 (paperback) | ISBN 9781475861334 (epub)
Subjects: LCSH: Educational leadership. | Teacher-administrator relationships. | Effective teaching.
Classification: LCC LB2806 .J5944 2022 (print) | LCC LB2806 (ebook) | DDC 371.2/03—dc23/eng/20220622
LC record available at https://lccn.loc.gov/2022020876
LC ebook record available at https://lccn.loc.gov/2022020877

This book is dedicated to all of the students who have been in my leadership classes. They all know if they are to become great instructional leaders, they must dedicate time for working with teachers to help them improve their instructional skills. They must remember that *Instruction Is the Heart of Learning*.

Contents

Foreword		ix
Preface		xi
Acknowledgments		xiii
Introduction		1
1	Redefining Instructional Leadership	5
2	Teachers' Expectations of Principals as School Leaders	21
3	Students' Assessment of Quality Teaching	35
4	Is There an Instructional Leader in the School?	51
5	Teachers Need More Supervision, Not Evaluation	65
6	Redefining Professional Development		85
7	Movement and Learning in the Classroom	101
About the Authors		115

Foreword

Schools and school-system leaders have spent—and continue to spend—considerable time, effort, and resources over the last decades to enhance and strengthen instructional leadership with the goal of enhancing student learning. Often these efforts take the form of instructional "supervision" and "evaluation" programs and tools intended to assist teachers in maximizing student potential. Given this continued huge investment, a reasonable query is the extent to which such programs have been effective.

Jones and Henry forcefully argue that success has been elusive and suggest that leaders should employ more innovative strategies and tactics for enhancing student learning. Blending considerable practical application with ample support from empirical and scholarly literature, they bring a fresh, invigorating perspective to a body of work that has received significant attention in both the scholarship and in practice over many years.

No stone is left unturned as the authors delve into critical instructional leadership areas such as instructional supervision, systems of teacher evaluation, professional development, and movement in the classroom (which has received more recent attention in the literature). The comprehensiveness of this book as well as the skilled manner by which the authors deftly merge theory with practice render the book a must-read for education leaders, as well as students of educational leadership.

—Jeffrey Maiden, PhD
Professor, educational administration, curriculum and supervision (EACS)
Senior researcher and director, Institute for the
Study of Education Finance (ISEF)
Codirector, EACS Online

University of Oklahoma Department of Educational
Leadership and Policy Studies
820 Van Vleet Oval
Norman, OK 73019

Preface

This book has been written during an extremely rough time for all teachers, students, and educational leaders. During this time, schools in our country have been, at times, devastated by the covid virus. It has had a devastating impact on teaching and learning. However, in spite of this crisis, education has persisted and school leaders, teachers, students, and the community at large gave the best they could to support this great profession. This book is primarily focused on instructional improvement and how school leaders must function as instructional leaders to help teachers improve their overall performance in teaching.

Redefining instructional leadership is a must, and the central theme of this book is that principals must be instructional leaders; it is written from a practitioner's point of reference. Throughout this book, the reader will understand that an instructional leader's top priority is to build **R**elationships, and with those relationships that are built, the leader will earn the **T**rust from their teachers that will give them the **I**nfluence they need to lead them to better levels of performance—and better performance leads to greater depths of student achievement.

Creating RTI supports and frames the practices of teachers and how they relate specifically to student learning. In addition, readers will also understand why school leaders should work with their teachers in helping them become great teachers; they will also learn that the best way to build positive relationships requires instructional leaders to be in classrooms supporting and working with teachers, helping them in all they do. This is something the great instructional leaders do, and it is time for all school leaders to see this as a necessity and perform the tasks and responsibilities associated with being that great school leader.

The content of this book has grown from years of frustration of listening to teachers, school leaders, and students discuss how they believe schools can improve. Indeed, schools can improve, but schools need people making the correct decisions about what they do and how they do it. This seems to be so foreign to what schools should be and how they can improve every component of what they are to do, and that is to improve teaching that fosters greater depths of student achievement.

This book will be great for new instructional leaders and a refresher for those who currently are in those positions. This book goes far beyond simply stating theory and summarizing research about what schools need from instructional leaders. It places great emphasis on what instructional leaders should do and how to do it.

It seems that in many cases, the focus in many educational leadership programs around the country are failing in preparing their students to be proficient in analyzing teaching and how to work with teachers in schools to be truly outstanding instructors.

This book clearly explains the steps instructional leaders must take, learn, and put into practice if their desire is to be a truly dynamic instructional leader, and one that will have a great and positive impact on teaching and learning. It is the hope for those who read this book that they will put into practice those things that will truly have a positive impact on instructional leadership and greater performance from teachers and students.

Acknowledgments

First of all, I cannot express enough thanks to Dr. Brittany Hott for her help and support. From the beginning of this book, she helped me greatly in making sure I had everything in proper order before things were sent to Rowman & Littlefield. I owe her my sincere thanks. I want to thank my graduate assistant who is coauthor of this book. Her understanding and completion of chapter seven is truly outstanding. In addition, I want to express my deepest thanks and gratitude to Dr. Tom Koerner, vice president and publisher for education issues for Rowman & Littlefield. While experiencing difficult challenges, he provided me additional time to complete the book.

Lastly, my completion of this book could not have been completed without the support of my wife, who graciously allowed me to spend an enormous amount of time working on my laptop to complete this very important project.

Introduction

This book will be a great resource for new instructional leaders, as it is seriously needed today in assisting those who desire to become instructional leaders of schools; it can also serve as a refresher for those who are already in school leadership positions. It seems that many who are serving as principals have forgotten or never learned what is truly needed from them to lead schools more effectively.

This book goes far beyond simply stating theory and summarizing research about what schools need from instructional leaders. It places great emphasis on what instructional leaders should do and how to do it. If school leaders will use the concepts presented and discussed in this book as a resource and guide for school improvement, improvement can happen.

As school leaders put into practice what they have learned from the content presented in this book, they will find themselves having a huge impact on teaching and learning, and that means they must help teachers perform better in the classroom—and when doing so, that will translate into greater depths of student achievement.

In addition, this book is organized to provide support and help for teachers and school leaders and to provide them usable tools as resources they need and can use that will give them the guidance and direction for overall school improvement. This book addresses numerous issues and problems that are prevalent in schools today; therefore, many of these issues and problems are addressed multiple times for emphasis.

This is not because the authors have forgotten what they previously said, but it is so those in school level instructional leadership positions can realize "if it is to be, it is up to me." This means if dynamic school improvements are made, it is up to those in school leadership positions to make them. The following statements reflect what readers will learn from each chapter.

CHAPTER ONE: REDEFINING INSTRUCTIONAL LEADERSHIP

This chapter capitalizes on the authors having over sixty years of experience working with teachers and assisting them in achieving excellence of instruction in the classroom. These years of experience have allowed the authors to develop the following overall mission for instructional leaders. That mission is this: Instructional leaders must understand that greater student achievement depends on those leaders within schools and the conditions they *must* create to ensure that professional growth and teaching expertise are maximized. The opening chapter introduces RTI and translates current educational theory and cutting-edge practices that generate great results from teachers, students, and instructional leaders.

CHAPTER TWO: TEACHERS' EXPECTATIONS OF PRINCIPALS AS SCHOOL LEADERS

The concept of instructional leadership has gradually emerged over the past few decades to mean different things to different people. Without great teachers, there will not be great schools. Therefore, if a school's instruction is not of top quality, so goes the quality of the students who go to the next grade level or those who graduate from the schools. Instructional leaders must emphasize instructional improvement. Therefore, it is imperative that instructional leaders be able to help teachers improve their instruction.

As instructional leaders, they must be totally committed and involved in the instructional process. Teachers are asking for help and want to get out of the isolation they operate in—and are expecting and desiring better support from those charged to help them. This chapter explains how school leaders can help teachers get out of this isolation and provide them the support they deserve and desperately need.

CHAPTER THREE: STUDENTS' ASSESSMENT OF QUALITY TEACHING

One might ask if students have the expertise to help teachers get better. Those who understand this concept, say "yes, they do," and this chapter is dedicated to what students are saying they need from their teachers to help them learn. Students do know for themselves what helps them learn. They may not know the pedagogical terminology, but they do know what they need to help them be more successful in the classroom.

Listening to what students say about teaching and their learning may seem a radical approach from the way most schools are structured, but if educators value learning, then it seems right that educators should listen to those who are recipients of what is being taught to them. This chapter shares with readers what students are saying they need from their teachers and how this need can help them in their learning.

CHAPTER FOUR: IS THERE AN INSTRUCTIONAL LEADER IN THE SCHOOL?

Today, more than ever, the practice of instructional supervision has had such an urgent need to help teachers excel in the classroom to become dynamic teachers. It is essential that educators—especially those who consider themselves to be instructional leaders—focus on helping teachers improve their instructional skills. This means that instructional leaders must be intentional about this process and work with teachers to improve all aspects related to teaching.

Readers of this chapter will find out that if the desire is to improve the essence of teaching, then it is the professional responsibility to do those things that instructional leaders should know and be able to do that support this. This chapter will focus on the intentionality and practical strategies and practices that can help accomplish this in schools.

CHAPTER FIVE: TEACHERS NEED MORE SUPERVISION, NOT EVALUATION

The field of supervision of instruction badly needs to be revisited. It is not about models that currently are used today to assess teaching. There are many things instructional leaders can do and use that provides greater insight into what teachers do in the classroom and how they do it. When providing support and help for teachers, instructional leaders must know what to do and how to do it, but many fail in this area.

Quality supervision and evaluation must incorporate analysis and reflection of teaching and give significant information and feedback about how to improve the essence of teaching that supports greater depths of student engagement and learning. This chapters explains how to do this correctly, and it is hoped school leaders will follow the steps defined in this chapter. If so, they will see greater improvements in their leadership skills as well as better teaching and learning.

CHAPTER SIX: REDEFINING PROFESSIONAL DEVELOPMENT

As an instructional leader, it is critical to find time during the work environment to help teachers develop professionally. It is important for teachers to understand time will be set aside and dedicated to professional learning. This work-embedded professional learning should be an expectation and an opportunity for colleagues to collaboratively discuss teaching and learning. It is sad to say, but this is not done very much today.

Most professional development that is provided to teachers is usually about some program or model that is supposed to support teaching and learning, but teachers say this is not sufficient in helping them learn the things they need to support their teaching and the needs of their students. This chapter redefines professional development that relates specifically to what teachers need and how schools must provide for those needs.

CHAPTER SEVEN: MOVEMENT AND LEARNING IN THE CLASSROOM

Over the past few decades, physical education and recess continue to steadily decline in schools and in homes across America. Simultaneously, there is an increase in the expectation for schools to encourage students to live a healthy and active lifestyle. It is therefore extremely important that school leaders and teachers understand this and work together with parents (to help them work with their children) to help them live healthy lifestyles that support their learning.

Frequently, studies tell us that students who are more active demonstrate sharpened focus, faster cognitive processing, and more successful memory retention than students who are less active. This chapter's focus is on how school leaders and teachers can accomplish this in schools and how it can have a positive impact on learning and social and emotional skills.

Finally, it is hoped that readers of this book will gain further knowledge regarding how to become great instructional leaders and will be able to utilize what they learn to help their teachers become master teachers, and for them to understand that instructional leaders must become master teachers as well. Teachers and school leaders need help, and this book provides them the tools and resources they need that will give them the guidance and direction for overall school improvement.

Chapter One

Redefining Instructional Leadership

There is no doubt about it: the American educational system has been undergoing some significant transformations in the past few decades. To maneuver through these changes and those to come, it is imperative that school leaders examine their beliefs and feelings about instructional leadership more rigorously than ever before. Since the 1980s, school-level instructional leadership has changed significantly and many of those changes have caused schools to digress in many areas; many believe this is due to a lack of focus from the principal as the instructional leader schools so desperately need.

Every chapter in this book relates specifically to several issues that are faced by teachers, students, and school leaders. There are times readers of this book may say to themselves, "this particular comment or statement has already been made," and that may be true, but there are times when things need to be restated and emphasized for a deeper and more thorough understanding. In addition, this book dedicates the last chapter to addressing the importance of assisting students in their learning endeavors using movement in the classroom, such as brain breaks, yoga, and action-based learning.

If schools are to succeed in the years to come, school leaders must not only have their heads in the right places, but their hearts as well. This will require many in school leadership positions to redefine what their functions should be if school leadership is their pursuit. They must keep the major focus at the forefront, and this focus must be dedicated to improving *teaching* and *learning*.

Quality teaching is the underlying principle that makes a school great. At the same time, educators must never forget that quality teaching must be nurtured by great leadership. Instructional leaders must understand that greater student achievement depends on leaders within the schools and the conditions they must create to ensure that professional growth and teaching expertise are maximized.

This will require instructional leaders to develop a better and different way of looking at and thinking about what is currently done in schools today. Many researchers and even some school leaders are saying the challenges in today's schools are increasing in frequency, complexity, and intensity—therefore, influencing a demand for a new level of excellence from school leaders.[1] With that in mind, instructional leaders must focus on excellence in everything they do that relates to instructional improvement.

Particularly compelling—especially considering some of the teacher evaluation systems so prevalent in schools today—is our role of inspiring teachers to do a great job of teaching and become leaders in the classroom. It should be apparent to all educators that good teaching matters, it is the *sine qua non* of schooling; in fact, good teaching is what instructional leadership is about: finding ways to improve teaching and learning.[2]

For years, an enormous amount of time has been spent attempting to motivate teachers with bribes and threats. This must change! It is time school leaders learn the value of intrinsic motivation, in which motivation—as well as its reward—comes from doing an excellent job. It is time to create schools in which school leaders and teachers work together and inspire each other. This inspiration should then be utilized in creating an environment where students have a desire to learn. All of this starts with quality school leadership.

There are three questions that must be asked about instructional leaders and those who are leading schools, and they are:

- What makes people want to follow the school leader?
- Why do people reluctantly comply with one school leader while passionately following another anywhere?
- What separates leadership theorists from those who really can lead effectively?

The answer to these questions lies in the character of the individual leading, not in the knowledge and application of leadership theory. At its essence, leadership touches the heart and soul of everyone in the school. Therefore, leading is based on an emotional connection rather than a rational one. Leadership is about making connections, and it requires instructional leaders to be focused on their purpose and intense in their beliefs.

It must also be understood that success does not depend on title, but rather on the choices that are made based on the principles that leaders value and hold dear. These principles must be based on the relationships school leaders make with those individuals who are in and outside of the school.

It has been said that management techniques are essential and that is certainly true, but what matters is leadership. To understand leadership, it must be understood that it is not about a *system* of leadership that can be learned and then implemented. There are no systems or theories that can be installed that would help those in school leadership positions effectively lead their school. Therefore, instructional leadership is an art that must be learned and not a theory that is put into practice.

School leaders must learn to attract followers/teachers for pragmatic reasons. They must offer them something they feel they need, even if they help them create that need. It is impossible to give school leaders a system (or to teach them about one) that can be imposed on a school or group of followers that will cause them to accept the person as their leader. Leadership must be done by the leader. School leaders must lead and learn how. This means that leadership is about helping those closest to the educators become better.

Many individuals believe that leadership can be conferred, but this is certainly not true, especially as it relates to instructional leaders in schools. School leaders must be accepted as the leader, and if they do not know how to lead, teachers will have little respect for them and no desire to follow them. Some school leaders may think they are in control because they have been appointed to the highest leadership position in the school, but great and real leadership is much more than demonstrating authority.

It takes more than having a degree in educational leadership. Leading a school requires school leaders to perform in ways that school staff and others will gladly and confidently follow them. This also means completing tasks in the school through the help and dedicated support of those following the leader. There are certain qualities that great school leaders have that separate them apart from others who are not considered great. The following are four things that can help a school leader become great.

A GREAT SCHOOL LEADER IS RESOLUTE

They cannot be afraid to take a risk and even make a mistake. Great school leaders fully understand that greatness is sometimes founded on making mistakes. This is in line with what the great Olympic Champion Bob Richards once said: "It may sound strange, but many champions are made champions by setbacks."[3] School leaders should not make decisions in haste but should thoroughly think through decisions that must be made and remember there will be setbacks.

It must be understood that many decisions that are made can have a positive or negative impact on those who are following them, and it would be best to make school-based decisions after carefully looking at all the ramifications and potential impact these decisions could have on the school. It is sad to say, but many do not do this because they make decisions without carefully analyzing the potential consequences of those decisions.

Great school leaders also must understand sometimes they have to leap into the unknown and that means they may risk a lot to make the school's dreams come true. They must also be able to get others to take the leap with them. This tends to separate leaders from each other. There are numerous people with outstanding talent in school leadership positions today who are afraid to take that risk.

It must be remembered and understood that out of risk taking comes strength to move forward, and that allows the school to improve in all facets related to leading, teaching, and learning. The school leader will make mistakes—perhaps some huge ones!

Making mistakes will require school leaders to make changes in the ways they are doing things to get the results that are needed to improve schools. This will require school leaders to make shifts in the way they lead and in the things they do. This *leadership-shifting* gives school leaders the ability to make a leadership change that will positively enhance the growth of the school.[4] However, the leader cannot afford to make the biggest mistake of all—that is, the mistake of doing nothing and not making decisions that will afford teachers and students the ability to excel in all they do.

A GREAT SCHOOL LEADER IS POSITIVE

Anything less than being positive will kill the leader and the school. Positivism gives fresh breath and life to the school and others will gladly follow a leader who is positive and intentional about leading them in directions they think they cannot go. This type of positivism is always moving forward and leading to results that lead to meaning.

A GREAT SCHOOL LEADER IS ENDURING

There will always be individuals who say, "this cannot be done." In life, many things have been accomplished without the help and support of others. School leaders must be stubbornly persistent to be the best at what they do, and they will find by doing this, things will be completed in a timely manner.

A GREAT SCHOOL LEADER IS FAITHFUL

School leaders who have goals and ideas about excellence for schools also have listened to others who have gone down the same road and have learned to persevere. This perseverance comes with dedication and faith that brings the school to life, and everyone in the school can reap the benefits of that greatness. With this comes great results, and that is what is needed today in our schools.

It is important to know that everything rises and falls on leadership and leadership develops from the inside out, just as schools do. This means becoming a school leader requires that leaders must become what they should be on the inside, and that will help them become what they need to be on the outside. This also applies to the school.

The bottom line is this: people will desire to follow them, and when this happens, the school leader and the teachers they are leading will accomplish great things. For many people, this is a complete change, and some just cannot change. That is why it must be understood that change is certain, but growth is optional. This means that school leaders must learn to grow as change takes place. This concept also applies to teachers.

LEARNING TO LEAD

For years educators and policy makers have talked about school reform, and many reforms have been implemented for the express purpose for improving schools. But maybe it is time to start discussions regarding school leadership reform. If schools are to be effective, so must the leadership of the schools be. It must be understood that regarding all the factors that contribute to what students learn in schools, leadership is second only to instruction.[5]

Those who are in positions of leading schools today must be prepared to lead in meaningful ways that can direct and mold schools through the change and efforts that will provide a positive impact on every individual in the school. This is specifically in line with what great leadership is all about because great instructional leaders understand and know what needs to be done and how to do it.[6] If change is necessary, then the primary focus should be directed to improving instruction and student achievement.

It is crucial that all school leaders understand and know that if schools make the kind of changes necessary to enhance the academic achievement of all students, they will have to keep their focus on instruction; they must also be able to create a safe environment with teachers by using dialogue rather than dictates.[7] This fosters the building of great relationships with their teachers. Some may find this very hard to do, but those who perform this in this manner get great results from their teachers and the school thrives.

Real school leadership requires leaders to put themselves in a position where teachers will place their complete confidence in the school leader's skills and abilities and gladly follow them. As a leader in any school, it is important to learn and study what great leaders do and have done.

One thing that must be learned is that great school leaders must learn to surround themselves with great teachers and work with them to help them become even greater. For those individuals whose desire is to become a great school leader, they must understand and potentially model those great school leaders who have paved the way and recognize that leadership involves three things: relationships, trust, and influence (RTI).

Once great relationships are developed, teachers will begin to trust the leader; then (and only then) will the school leader have the influence that is needed to lead teachers somewhere. Understanding how RTI works and applying its principles will also build confidence and competence in those doing the leading. This is in complete compliance with what great leadership is all about, and if school leaders do not have influence, they will never be able to lead others.[8]

Several chapters in this book will address what this chapter refers to as the *four dimensions for instructional improvement.* Many may think that instructional improvement only relates to what teachers do in the classroom and how school leaders work with teachers to address these instructional practices. There is no simple way to assess the quality of instruction. However, by thinking carefully about the purpose of teacher evaluation and by crafting multiple methods for doing this, an evaluation/assessment system can be devised that is reliable, valid, and fair.[9]

Equally important is the process of discussing and crafting evaluation/assessment systems that focus attention on all the practices that are associated with and support quality teaching. This is a culture that should be created in every school if schools expect to exceed in all aspects associated with teaching and learning. The most important consideration in assessing and evaluating teaching, both for improvement purposes and for personnel decisions, is the use of multiple methods involving multiple sources of data. This also means the instructional leader must be assessed as relates to their performance as instructional leaders. If instruction is to continuously improve in schools, it must be viewed from different dimensions. These four dimensions for instructional improvement are:

- teacher-to-teacher dimension
- student-to-teacher dimension

- principal-to-teacher dimension
- teacher-to-principal dimension

Taking a closer look at these four dimensions requires educators to ask five questions that relate to the overall process associated with quality improvement in schools.

- Does the school/district use multiple methods for assessing/evaluating teaching?
- Is the system reliable, valid, and fair, and does it focus on all practices associated with instructional improvement?
- Is the system valued by teachers, students, and school leaders?
- Is the school improving in all four dimensions relating to the practices that improve instruction?
- Is it a once-and-done process, or is it a continuous process that focuses on improvement of instruction and the four dimensions associated with it?

To ensure the assessment/evaluation system adopted by the school district is credible and acceptable, faculty should be involved in the process of its development. This is not the case most of the time, but those teachers and school leaders who are going to live with the results should be involved in the developmental process of what is used to assess all components relating to instructional practices. Schools utilizing the current systems today have not realized the huge benefit that can come from the involvement of all stakeholders developing an evaluation/assessment system. Things to consider in the development process are as follows:

- criteria need to be determined by everyone;
- instruments used should be standards-based;
- since different disciplines require different methods and settings for instruction, this requires different methods and criteria for evaluation and assessing instructional practices; and
- teaching evaluation systems can be flexible to accommodate diversity in instructional methods (e.g., lecture, discussion, lab, small/large group interaction).

TEACHER-TO-TEACHER DIMENSION

Teacher colleagues who have expertise in the discipline, being taught and trained in what to observe, can provide valuable information through classroom visits, review course materials and instructional contributions. At the same time, they should not limit themselves to those who have expertise in the same content area or in what they might observe while in another teacher's classroom.. The idea is to get faculty to collaborate about teaching and learning based on direct observation.

This formative approach should be done more if schools really desire to improve the essence of instruction that impacts student learning. Allowing teachers to observe each other and to collaboratively work with each other can provide the following benefits:

- teachers can provide valuable information through classroom visits;
- teachers can assess course materials, techniques, handouts, assignments, graded exams, graded papers, etc.; and
- teachers can provide valuable information regarding classroom management techniques.

A teacher colleague's observation of such aspects of teaching—appropriateness of materials and methods and breadth and depth of material covered—can offer a more informed appraisal of the instructor's mastery of and teaching of course content. Many believe that peer observation has enjoyed great success as a strategy for improved instruction. The teacher-to-teacher observation process is enhanced when, prior to classroom visits, colleagues review the course-related materials and discuss course goals and class objectives with the instructor.

STUDENT-TO-TEACHER DIMENSION

Most schools do not allow for student input regarding instructional practices that relate to their learning, and in many cases, students can provide valuable information on the extent to which a teacher appears prepared for class—if they communicate clearly, stimulate interest, demonstrate enthusiasm for teaching, and if they show respect for students. Research in this area shows that student responses on this dimension are valid and reliable.[10]

In addition, students are more than able to share with teachers about how they learn and what teachers can do to stimulate their learning. Periodic student feedback throughout the year is particularly helpful for teaching improvement purposes, but it must be understood students are less able to judge the knowledge of the instructor or scholarly content and currency of a course. However, it could greatly benefit educators and students if students were given an opportunity to assess teacher performance. It is apparent that no one spends more time watching teachers at work than students, so it logically follows no one is in a better position to evaluate their performance as it relates to how they learn.[11]

PRINCIPAL-TO-TEACHER DIMENSION

This process in most schools today appears to be broken. One hears teachers all the time say, "The principal is seldom or never in my classroom, but still evaluates my teaching performance." Surely this is not what schools need, and in most cases, the assessment of instruction needs immediate improvements by those who are charged to assess it. It must be understood that if value is placed on quality instruction, then it should be assessed because it is valued. Teachers deserve better instructional analysis, and it is the school leader's responsibility to provide it.

For years, research has been conducted about what constitutes what great school leaders are and should be able to do in supporting teaching and learning. From this research, several instructional leadership suggestions have been developed that are still applicable but, in most cases, are not followed. Research in this area suggests there are multiple traits that are associated with strong and successful school leadership and these traits suggest that great instructional leaders should be able to:

- create a climate for high expectations;
- function as an instructional leader;
- consult with teachers regularly;
- create a climate in the school characterized by respect for teachers, students, and community;
- place a priority on instructional issues; and
- continuously monitor student progress.[12]

This clearly suggests that school instructional leaders should have high expectations and focus on the principal-to-teacher dimension more than ever before. This also suggests that communication with teachers is necessary, and being in classrooms, supporting what they do, is crucial; this fosters relationship building that creates trust that will give the school leader the influence needed to lead.

TEACHER-TO-PRINCIPAL DIMENSION

It seems fair to say if principals get to assess teachers for their teaching performance, then teachers should be allowed to assess principals for their performance as instructional leaders. It is understood that evaluating the performance of principals can be challenging since most principals have multiple functions as leader of the building. However, when it comes to their performance as an instructional leader and their working with teachers to improve instructional practices, teachers do have the ability and do possess skills for doing this.

Clearly, educators and even policy makers should understand it is impossible to expect school leaders to improve if their gathering and acting on the right information about their effectiveness as leaders of learning is not done.[13] Again, teachers are in the perfect position to do this, but most school districts do not afford teachers the opportunity to assess school leaders for their performance as instructional leaders.

If the school leader is ever assessed, it is usually done by someone from the district office who has limited time to assess the school leader's skills and abilities as instructional leaders. These individuals may be responsible for evaluating principals in the district, but they can only observe a small part of what the leader of the school does. District personnel are not in the school every day as teachers are, and they probably never appear in classrooms when teachers are being assessed or assisted by the principal regarding improvement of instruction. When schools practice these four dimensions, there is a great chance that teaching and learning will improve, and the overall performance from teachers and instructional leaders will also be enhanced.

It is necessary that schools practice these four dimensions if excellence relating to these instructional practices is the desire of the school. However, many school leaders believe they have too many priorities that are in conflict with each other and that causes them to falter in being the instructional leader they should be. It is imperative that school districts make sure that school leaders have sufficient time to spend in the classroom working on important issues that relate specifically to what is the primary purpose and what is to be accomplished in classrooms.

This issue has been addressed when numerous principals were interviewed who had voluntarily left their principalships after serving from two to more-than-ten years. Reasons provided by these principals for their decisions included:

- a discrepancy between the level of accountability expected of principals and the lack of influence they really have over many factors affecting school success;
- a sense of being isolated when dealing with challenges;
- a workload that sometimes seems simply not doable; and

- preservice training that left them feeling unprepared for the challenges of the job.[14]

After reviewing these reasons for leaving school leadership positions, I found it apparent that school districts are failing to create the conditions that make it possible for school leaders to lead school improvements effectively.[15] What happens instead is that in some districts, administrators attempt to exert complete control over every phase of instruction and school operations.

They try to own all the problems and enforce all solutions from the top down. In other districts, administrators turn all the problems over to the school leader, offering little or no sense of direction or support—just a demand for results. This is truly a problem today in schools.

CONCLUDING THOUGHTS

This chapter and the entirety of this book suggest that school leadership should be redefined. In addition, a great amount of time is dedicated to what instructional leaders should do in schools to improve every facet associated with instruction. It is time for school leaders to stop making excuses that keep them out of classrooms, helping teachers improve every aspect associated with teaching and learning.

Today's educational climate is marked by an increased focus on improving student achievement, and school leaders are frequently at the center of this increased focus. The organizational, managerial, and instructional roles of school leaders are often competing for time, and as a result, instructional leadership that is so needed in schools is being neglected.

It is apparent that most educators simply have not defined what effective school leadership is and how it is demonstrated in schools today. It takes commitment and understanding of how to design schools into great teaching and learning environments. This should be the commitment of all school leaders, and it must start with those in positions of leadership. This means that authentic and dynamic leadership should be an absolute for all schools. This must take place if schools are to become dynamic places where teaching and learning take place.

This is in complete compliance with the National Association of Elementary School Principals as they recently said:

> Principals can no longer simply be administrators and managers. They must be instructional leaders focused on improving student achievement. They must be the force that creates collaboration and cohesion around school learning goals and the commitment to achieve those goals.[16]

This statement is very clear and to the point, and it simply cannot be achieved unless a change is made in the leadership understanding and direction that school leaders must make to meet the needs of schools. As stated numerous times throughout this book, the most important thing school leaders can do is to be in classrooms.

If this does not occur, those designated as school leaders are failing their teachers, students, and the education profession. Literature regarding school instructional leadership for years has emphasized that quality instructional leadership is crucial for school improvement.

This literature has been valuable in suggesting improvements that are desperately needed. It must be asked why these improvements have not been made in so many of the schools today, and the only answer is that many school leaders have failed in this endeavor. It must be understood that instructional leaders are responsible and should be held accountable for developing and supporting teachers and providing them with ample opportunities for growth.

Instructional leaders must focus on improving their practice and must think about their goal of improving instruction that supports greater student outcomes. Therefore, to have better student outcomes, school leaders must know how to make instruction a priority at their school. In addition, school leaders should allow and foster teacher ownership over their own teaching.[17]

It is apparent that instructional leaders should focus on creating conditions where teachers want to and can improve themselves.[18] This is something that can and should be practiced and nurtured in schools, but again, it starts when instructional leaders create this climate in schools by being in classrooms working with teachers and demonstrating how these conditions can be created and cultivated with teachers.

The idea of someone who is a principal demonstrating the precepts as an instructional leader is not a new concept. However, the principal as instructional leader needs the support from the district office to make this their number one priority. District leaders must recognize that each of their schools need an instructional leader who supports and can enhance teaching and learning. Without this, teachers and students will not flourish in the classroom.

In addition, it must be asked if school leaders are being held accountable for improvements in teaching and learning. If they are to be held accountable for making sure teaching is excellent and greater depths of academic achievement are attained by all students, they should be given more freedom to do this as well as the support that enhances these two major functions of schools.

This support from the district office is crucial, and it is an absolute that teachers see this as a commitment and know it is the school districts' number one priority. If this does not happen, instruction will be less effective and so will student learning in schools.

As individuals find themselves in instructional leadership positions, it is imperative to learn the internality of what leading is all about. This simply means that school leaders must be *intentional* about the decisions they make because these decisions can have a positive or negative impact on those they are trying to lead.

This should cause those pursuing school leadership to reflect on themselves first, before beginning the leadership journey, and the actions they may have to take when working with others. This reflection should cause instructional leaders to realize it is not about themselves but those they are attempting to lead and serve. Far too many individuals in instructional leadership positions fail to realize this simple leadership function.

This also means they may need to improve *themselves* first. This may involve change and change is very hard for some. This intentional reflection on self can be a great challenge for some because, at times, it is difficult (and sometimes impossible) to lead others unless the self is fixed first. School leaders must become a student of learning about what great leaders do and how they do it, but most of all, how to influence lives positively and seek to help others achieve excellence.

Truly, individuals who are dedicated to becoming great instructional leaders cannot be consumed with the self. Leadership is about leading and that alone places instructional leaders in a position of leading others to a better place of understanding and greater success for schools.

At the same time, it is important for every person who considers himself or herself an instructional leader to bring to the school certain values that are transparent and can be shared by everyone in the school. These values are what inspires leading and they shape leadership direction, provide the distinctive character of those leading, and determine the passion used in leading the school. This passion can and will influence others to follow.[19] Based on this, it is apparent that having strong and acceptable values could give instructional leaders the personal capacity that is necessary and also would help in defining the leader as being credible.

School leaders must understand what great teaching looks like and how it can magnify student learning—and what steps must be taken to improve both. Without this understanding of how to improve both, those responsible for leading in these two areas will fail as instructional leaders. It must be clearly understood that schools are about teaching and learning, and all activities outside of this are secondary to these basic goals.[20]

Supporting this should not be a problem when the school administrator is an educational leader who promotes the success of all students by advocating, nurturing, and sustaining a school culture and instructional program conducive to student learning and teacher professional growth.[21] Finally, it must be understood that all aspects associated with becoming a great school leader take time and is a learned process; the steps related to this process are steps that many in school leadership positions are not willing or know how to take.

However, those who do know how and take these steps will find themselves to be in a truly remarkable place, and this book can help school leaders learn how to take those steps and improve their leadership skills. It will assist potential leaders in determining if becoming an instructional leader is what they want to pursue. At the same time, their school will flourish, and teachers will achieve great things in the classroom—as well as their students!

NOTES

1. Green, R. L. (2005). *Practicing the art of leadership* (2nd ed.). Upper Saddle River, NJ: Pearson Merrill Prentice Hall.

2. Hoy, W., & Hoy, A. (2013). *Instructional leadership: A research-based guide to learning in Schools* (4th ed.). Boston, MA: Allyn and Bacon.

3. AZ Quotes. (2021). *Bob Richard Quote.* Retrieved August 22, 2021 from https://www.azquotes.com/quote/1319732.

4. Maxwell, J. (2019). *Leader shift: 11 essential changes every leader must embrace.* New York, NY: Harper Collins.

5. Siccone, F. (2012). *Essential skills for effective school leadership.* Boston, MA: Pearson.

6. Findley, B., & Findley, D. (1992). Effective schools: The role of the principal. *Contemporary Education, 63 (2),* 102–4.

7. Supovitz, J. A., & Poglinco, S. M. (2001). *Instructional leadership in standards-based reform.* Retrieved May 9, 2021 from https://www.researchgate.net/publication/265273390_Instructional_Leadership_in_a_Standards-Based_Reform.

8. Maxwell, J. (2002). *Leadership 101.* Nashville, TN: Thomas Nelson.

9. Merriam, S. B., & Bierema, L. L. (2013). *Adult learning: Linking theory and practice.* San Francisco, CA: Jossey-Bass.

10. Jones, J., & Henry, M. (2019). Students' Assessment of Teacher Quality: Recommendations for Improvement. *Southeast Journal of Educational Administration, 19* (3), 1–16.

11. LaFee, S. (2014). Student evaluating teachers. *School Administrator, 71* (3), 17–25.

12. Persell, C., & Cookson, P. (1982). The effect of principals in action. *The Effective Principal: A Research Summary, 4,* 28–35.

13. *Assessing the effectiveness of school leaders: New directions and new processes.* (March 2009). Retrieved August 18, 2020 from https://www.wallacefoundation.org/knowledge-center/Documents/Assessing-the-Effectiveness-of-School-Leaders.pdf.

14. Johnson, L. (2005). Why principals quit: There are many reasons why principals voluntarily leave the positions they worked so hard to earn. *National Association of Elementary School Principals, 84* (3), 21–23.

15. Bottoms, G., & Schmidt-Davis, J. (2010). The three essentials: Improving schools requires district vision, district and state support, and principal leadership. *Southern Regional Educational Board, 10* (16), ii. Retrieved from https://www.wallacefoundation.org/knowledge-center/Documents/Three-Essentials-to-Improving-Schools.pdf.

16. *Leading learning communities: Standards for what principals should know and be able to do (Executive summary).* (2008). National Association of Elementary School Principals, 2.

17. Martin, J. (2019). *Turning a school around.* Washington, DC: Rowman & Littlefield.

18. Steele, D., & Whitaker, T. (2019). *Essential truths for principals* (1st ed.). New York, NY: Routledge.

19. Ubben, C. G., Hughes, L.W., & Norris, C. J. (2007). *The principal: Creative leadership for effective schools* (6th ed.). Boston, MA: Pearson.

20. Hoy, A. W., & Hoy, W. K. (2003). *Instructional leadership: A learning-centered guide.* Boston, MA: Allyn and Bacon.

21. *Educational leadership policy standards.* (December 12, 2007). Retrieved September, 8, 2021 from https://www.atu.edu/cll/docs/elps_isllc2008.pdf.

Chapter Two

Teachers' Expectations of Principals as School Leaders

The concept of instructional leadership has gradually emerged over the past few decades to mean different things to different people. There are those who suggest that outstanding principals know if they have great teachers, they have a great school.[1]

Therefore, if a school's instruction is not of top quality, the quality of the students who graduate or move to the next school will not be what it should. This chapter directly relates to the first of the four dimensions for improving instructional practices. That practice is the principal-to-teacher dimension.

Principals must emphasize and even insist that teachers provide quality instruction. But more than that, it is imperative for principals to function as instructional leaders and be able to help teachers improve their instructional skills. Never has the field of instructional supervision faced such an urgent need to help teachers thrive in the classroom.[2]

Any person desiring to become an instructional leader must understand the commitment it takes to providing this and recognize it as an absolute; it cannot be minimized. It is crucial to provide the support teachers need for instructional improvement. Everything that is done in the classroom must focus on this. It is sad to say, but in many situations, this critical function of providing instructional leadership does not happen in schools today.

Principals must be the instructional leaders in schools, and if they are not instructional leaders, teachers and students will ultimately suffer. If principals want their schools to be high-achieving schools where teachers and students flourish, they must work with teachers to set instructional goals, make sure the curriculum is standards-based, assess instructional performance, and use data to make any necessary improvements.[3]

In leadership, balance is necessary; however, if the school is going to be a vibrant school where teachers teach with passion and students achieve to higher levels, it is imperative the principal lead with passion and be passionate about those aspects that make teaching and learning come alive.[4] Teachers are entitled to the best support instructional leaders can give them, and at the same time, to give their best to their own instructional improvement. Students are worth this, and this will be discussed in greater depth later in this book. Students do expect educators' best efforts.

This chapter focuses on the primary concerns teachers have relating specifically to how the principal should be the instructional leader of the school and should help them improve their instructional skills, as well as what principals can do to meet teachers' concerns regarding instructional practices. Teachers want to improve, and they want their students to be proficient in learning and able to apply the content they have learned to new learning, but sometimes teachers need direct assistance. However, for many teachers, they are not receiving this assistance that helps and supports the teaching that equates to better learning.

TEACHERS ARE BEGGING FOR ASSISTANCE

Teachers do have a desire for leaders of their schools to be able to provide instructional assistance. When assistance is not provided, it can cause great confusion and a feeling of isolation for teachers. In many schools, they are begging for help, and in many schools, the specific help they need is just not provided. Teachers are diligently asking for and desiring additional support from their principals, especially as it relates to assisting them with skills that could improve their overall instructional performance.

There appears to be several primary concerns teachers have that must not go unaddressed; ten of these concerns are as follows:

- My principal should find out any concerns I have and any problems I feel I am having.
- My principal should be in my classroom more than just to complete the required evaluation of me.
- My principal should involve me in deciding what they will observe and the types of data they will collect during an observational visit.
- My principal should help me translate my concerns into specific teaching behaviors that can be observed.
- My principal should be able to suggest methods I can use to gather my own data about my teaching.
- When in a conference with me, my principal should listen more than he or she talks.

- My principal should acknowledge what I say and show me they understand what I am saying.
- My principal should encourage me to consider alternative teaching techniques and explanations of classroom events.
- My principal should be able to demonstrate what quality teaching looks like through his or her own teaching.
- My principal should be able to relate my perceptions of the class to the objective observational data, which he or she collects during a visit.[5]

These concerns are relevant in many schools today and every instructional leader should continually ask themselves, What do my teachers need from me, and what must I do as an instructional leader to provide for those needs? To better assist teachers in their teaching skills as well as to assist instructional leaders, the survey in Textbox 2.1 can be tremendously beneficial if teachers are given the opportunity to complete it. Once completed, both principal and teacher can review the results, and both can work on areas needing improvement.

It is safe to say that teachers desire their principal to be proficient in all areas associated with those of an instructional leader who works to support and improve instruction. Even though some may consider this assumption to be unrealistic, it is tenable. Teachers do believe principals should be able to collect and use data and be able to assist them to a greater extent with instructional expertise.

TEXTBOX 2.1. JONES INSTRUCTIONAL BEHAVIOR QUESTIONNAIRE (JIBQ)

Please read each of the following descriptions of classroom supervisory activities and techniques. In the left margin, circle the response which most nearly describes the extent to which you believe the ideal principal would use this technique. In the right margin, please circle the response that most nearly describes the extent to which your present principal uses the technique.

The following are definitions of the responses:

1 = NEVER (at no time, under no conditions)
2 = SELDOM (in few instances, rarely, infrequently)
3 = SOMETIMES (occasionally, once in a while)
4 = USUALLY (commonly or ordinarily used)
5 = OFTEN (many times)

Ideal Principal						My Principal				
1	2	3	4	5	1. Meets with me prior to formal observation of my class.	1	2	3	4	5
1	2	3	4	5	2. Prior to a visit, finds out what my lesson plan objectives are and what strategies I plan to use during the visit.	1	2	3	4	5
1	2	3	4	5	3. Prior to a visit, finds out what I expect students to be doing during the visit.	1	2	3	4	5
1	2	3	4	5	4. Prior to a visit, finds out any concern I have and any problems I feel I am having.	1	2	3	4	5
1	2	3	4	5	5. Prior to a visit, involves me in deciding what he or she will observe and the type of data he or she will collect during the visit.	1	2	3	4	5
1	2	3	4	5	6. Prior to a visit, helps me translate my concerns into specific teaching behaviors that can be observed.	1	2	3	4	5
1	2	3	4	5	7. Prior to a visit, suggests a variety of observational techniques that he or she could use during a visit.	1	2	3	4	5
1	2	3	4	5	8. Suggests methods that I can use to gather my own data about my teaching without help from others.	1	2	3	4	5
1	2	3	4	5	9. Makes verbatim notes of selected parts of what I say and what students say during the visit.	1	2	3	4	5
1	2	3	4	5	10. Writes down my questions during the visit for later analysis.	1	2	3	4	5
1	2	3	4	5	11. Writes students' responses to my questions for later analysis.	1	2	3	4	5
1	2	3	4	5	12. Makes a chart to show patterns and amount of student response in class discussions.	1	2	3	4	5
1	2	3	4	5	13. Makes charts to show physical movements of me and/or my students during the visit.	1	2	3	4	5
1	2	3	4	5	14. Makes verbatim notes of selected parts of what I say and what students say during the visit.	1	2	3	4	5
1	2	3	4	5	15. Observes and makes notes about the behavior of a specific child if I have identified that child as a "problem" student.	1	2	3	4	5
1	2	3	4	5	16. Records his or her subjective feelings about whether the class is good or bad.	1	2	3	4	5

Ideal Principal						My Principal				
1	2	3	4	5	17. Meets with me after each visit to discuss what he or she observed.	1	2	3	4	5
1	2	3	4	5	18. Relates my perceptions of the class to the objective observational data that he or she collected during the visit.	1	2	3	4	5
1	2	3	4	5	19. Asks me questions during the conference that help me to clarify my opinions and feelings.	1	2	3	4	5
1	2	3	4	5	20. Encourages me to consider alternative teaching techniques and explanations of classroom events.	1	2	3	4	5
1	2	3	4	5	21. Listens more than he or she talks in a conference.	1	2	3	4	5
1	2	3	4	5	22. Encourages me to make inferences and to express my feelings and opinions about observational data that he or she collected.	1	2	3	4	5
1	2	3	4	5	23. Acknowledges what I say and shows me that he or she understands what I am saying	1	2	3	4	5
1	2	3	4	5	24. Gives praise and encouragement for specific growth in my teaching skill that he or she has observed.	1	2	3	4	5
1	2	3	4	5	25. Recommends resources such as books and training programs that deal with areas that have been observed.	1	2	3	4	5

WHAT INSTRUCTIONAL LEADERS MUST DO

Principals must ask themselves if they spend sufficient time in the classrooms working with teachers to help them improve their instructional skills. It is probably safe to say that many principals spend minimal time in the classroom and therefore are unable to observe teachers teaching, making it impossible to know what is taking place in the classroom. Many would suggest this means they are unable to help teachers become more successful and to demonstrate those skills that come with this success.

Many principals say they are not able to find sufficient time to work with teachers to assist them in those areas that relate to instructional improvement, and this is primarily because of managerial duties. As previously stated, balance is extremely important as it relates to the administrative functions. However, principals must be able to balance their work to incorporate all aspects associated with those of an instructional leader. This extremely important function for many principals seems to be missing and needs to be addressed.

Principals as instructional leaders are the key to seeing that student achievement is attained. This is supported over and over by research that indicates the principal's main responsibility is to serve as "another set of eyes," holding up the "mirror of practice" in which the teacher can examine specific classroom behaviors.[6] However, few principals perform in this capacity. It is indeed a disgrace and shame that "effective instructional leaders are distinctly in the minority."[7] This must change if the expectation of teachers is to be quality instructors and to give students in their classrooms the best instruction possible. For this to happen, the principal must provide proper guidance, leadership, and supervisory skills.

Through informal discussions, many principals will admit they simply are not able to dedicate the amount of time they would like to assist teachers with instructional practices. Personal observations in schools will verify this. In addition, after having hundreds of conversations with principals and teachers, it is safe to say principals do spend minimal time in the classroom and even less time working with teachers, helping them improve their instructional skills.

They seem to spend more time arranging for someone who is external to the school to come to the school and provide professional development or instructional support than providing it themselves. This arrangement might work if those who were brought in could stay on as professional developmental staff and understood how to help teachers improve their instructional skills, but that is usually not the case.

There are several schools across the nation and in other countries that have principals who engage themselves in the instructional process and spend considerable amounts of time in the classroom. At the same time, they continue to get the other work associated with the principalship completed in a timely manner. They see themselves as the instructional leader and spend considerable time working with teachers to improve their instructional skills.

Certain federal legislative acts have as a premise and emphasize the administrator's role as the instructional leader.[8] Understandably, the depth of knowledge a classroom teacher has regarding their content is not necessarily needed by the principal; however, principals do need to know good teaching when they observe it. This means principals as instructional leaders must be able to lead teachers to produce verifiable results in the classroom.

As previously stated, principals do not need to be experts in all curricular areas, but they must be able to observe that lessons taught are aligned properly with appropriate standards and that teachers exhibit quality teaching techniques, so all students can learn to achieve their fullest potential, and can understand and apply higher-order thinking skills.

This will aid students in being more engaged in collaborative conversations with teachers and other students about course content. These things are observable, but they require school leaders to be in classrooms observing these things. Principals are extremely important to the instructional process, and no other position has the ability to improve schools better than the principal.

It is believed all educators would probably agree that "good teaching matters"; in fact, it is the *sine qua non* of schooling. Good teaching is what instructional leadership is about: finding ways to improve teaching and learning."[9] This assertion is bolstered by findings that emerge from what are considered to be successful schools. Queen Elizabeth High School in Edmonton, Alberta, Canada, represents one of those schools where the principal takes teaching and learning seriously. This school and what they do will be discussed in depth later in this chapter.

It is clear when schools are functioning especially well and school achievement is high, much of the credit typically must go to the principal. Legislative leaders understood the importance, as well (U.S. Senate, 1970):

> In many ways, the school principal is the most important and influential individual in any school. . . . It is his leadership that sets the tone of the school, the climate for learning, the level of professionalism and morale of teachers, and the degree of concern for what students may or may not become. . . . If a school is a vibrant, innovative, child-centered place; if it has a reputation for excellence in teaching; if students are performing to the best of their ability; one can almost always point to the principal's leadership as the key to success.[10]

If this were thought to be true in 1970, it seems it would be true today. However, as suggested, it seems fewer school principals are willing to take the helm of their school and lead the way. This reality is indeed unfortunate because principals as instructional leaders are, first and foremost, responsible for promoting best teaching practices.[11] In many cases, this simply does not take place in schools today. Principals must continually be engaging their faculty in discussions about quality instruction and reflective practices.

If quality instruction is the heart of learning, one can surmise that if instruction improves, so does student achievement. The two go together, and there are only two ways to improve schools: hire better teachers or improve the teachers that are in schools today.[12] This comment makes sense, but most administrators spend much of their time searching for programs they believe will improve instruction and supposedly will benefit student achievement.

The principal can spend all year looking for programs they believe will solve problems and improve instructional practices, but when the year is over, the same problem still exists and not much will have been solved—and it will be repeated the following year. Most of the time, these programs will not achieve the improvement needed or the desired results.

Everyone seems to be looking for a silver bullet, but if such a panacea existed, then every school would be using it. It must be asked: Is there a silver bullet or that cure-all, that program or model, that will bring about the positive results everyone seems to be seeking? Is there a program that will help every child achieve to his or her fullest potential? The obvious answer to this is a resounding "no."

But the question remains: is there a silver bullet? Many believe there is a silver bullet, and it is the teacher. Therefore, it is the instructional leader's responsibility to see that each teacher under their guidance becomes the best teacher they can become. Once again, children are worth all educators' best efforts, and this includes the principal. Children are the reason why we have teachers and principals in schools, who must not fail to provide them with the best educational training that is available.

Again, it is imperative that school leaders support this claim about effective leadership and their endeavors do this, for these efforts of the principal are mission critical to what schools are all about and do.[13] Instruction itself has the largest influence on achievement, and educators' best efforts (in many cases) are insufficient—teachers and school leaders must make the necessary changes to see significant improvements are made.[14]

As further suggested by many researchers, teachers do indeed want to improve their instructional skills, and they do indeed desire assistance from their principal. Conversations with Pre-K–12 teachers will further verify that elementary school principals spend more time in the classroom than their secondary counterparts.

Additional researchers also verify this fact by stating most high school principals spend less time in the classroom than principals in elementary and middle schools for the express purpose of "observing classroom practices, promoting discussions about instructional issues, and emphasizing the use of test results for program improvement."[15] Others suggest that when principals conduct classroom observations, they have a "front-row seat" to observe what occurs during the teaching process, and this front-row seat is crucial and provides sufficient information that can be used to help teachers.[16]

It is a proven fact that if principals spend time in the classroom observing and working with teachers, it is the most significant predictor of a school's success. Queen Elizabeth High School in Edmonton, Alberta, Canada, has implemented a program that allows the principal to spend half of the day in the classroom.

The principal monitors and observes teaching and, at the same time, models effective teaching.[17] This shows principals functioning as instructional leaders and demonstrating to their teachers what great teaching looks like.

Principals performing as instructional leaders who work with teachers to improve instruction should know how to model and demonstrate what great teaching looks like. Edmonton Public Schools expect all principals to be in classrooms regularly and for them, that means daily. This school's system leaders show that it can be done.

While demonstrating that it can be done, they have also had positive results. For example, there have been improvements in student course completion, student behavior and conduct, the number of suspensions has dropped dramatically, and, yes, there have been greater depths of student achievement.

Teachers also report improved morale and greater support from the principal, and principals saw themselves as instructional leaders. This makes instructional leadership a major priority in their schools. This school system seems to be on the cutting edge of what every school should desire and what instructional leadership should be and look like in a school. Principals are in classrooms regularly assisting teachers. Teaching has improved and student achievement has increased greatly because of the combined work of principals and teachers.

Those in instructional leadership positions should want and desire learning to increase, student conduct to improve, and there to be greater depths of student achievement. This is brought about by being an instructional leader who spends quality time in classrooms, working with teachers and helping them improve the essence of instruction.

Edmonton Public Schools clearly support what it takes to be great as they continually place an emphasis on student outcomes and support supervision of instruction as an indispensable function that inspires good teaching and promotes student learning.[18]

Still, many questions remain: What does effective instruction look like? Can a principal have an impact on instructional improvement? How do teachers view the principal as an instructional leader? Do teachers desire help from their principal? Research in this area is extremely limited, but some studies are available that can lend support. One of the best studies was conducted with 809 teachers using questionnaires to describe the characteristics of principals.[19]

In this study, teachers define the characteristics of effective leaders, and they find that principals as instructional leaders should give feedback from classroom observations, demonstrate teaching techniques in the classroom, focus on specific and concrete teaching behaviors, participate in staff development, and encourage teachers to become peer coaches.

This study is extremely important and clearly defines what teachers need from their school leaders and, until this takes place in every school, we will continue having ineffective leadership and teaching that does not promote and support greater depths of student learning.

Teachers desire their principal to be proficient in all areas associated with those of an instructional leader who works to support and improve instruction. Even though some may consider this assumption to be unrealistic, it is tenable. Teachers do believe their principal should be able to collect and use data. Furthermore, teachers want principals to be instructional leaders who can assist them to a greater extent with instructional expertise.

One might say if principals do these things, they must be in classrooms numerous times during the school year. However, as research and conversations with teachers do verify, it seems apparent that "effective instructional leaders are distinctly in the minority."[20] Even informal walk-through observations have proven to show some benefits, but many instructional leaders would say the average drop-in visit is insufficient. Without continual conversations about instructional practices, not much in instructional improvement will be attained.

Many school principals perform the typical drop-in visit a few times a year without continuous discussion with teachers, and these formal observations are meant to assist teachers, but they usually lead to nothing related to instructional improvement. It is unfortunate when this happens because it diminishes what teacher improvement entails. The person who is an instructional leader will not just drop in but will make it their number one priority to be in classrooms.

In schools, the principals, who are functioning as the instructional leader, should set the tone for quality instruction. If teachers and principals can work together to improve instruction, then student achievement will be enhanced. They should work in consort with each other, even to the extent of designing better observational tools that might generate better data for both to observe. When this occurs in schools, it allows teachers and principals the opportunity to work together to improve the overall quality of instruction, and our children receive the benefits.

This is clearly supported by research conducted by NASSP and NAESP in *Leadership Matters*. This report clearly articulates that principals should guide schools to better teaching and learning, and it further suggests this is accomplished by being in classrooms, working to help teachers improve the essence of instruction.[21]

For clarification on instructional leaders and what they should do, it must be understood by them that instructional leadership is based on the conviction that learning should be given top priority, while everything else evolves around the enhancement of learning.[22]

This means that instructional leaders must be fully aware of what is taking place in every teacher's classroom, and that means there must be a physical presence in these classrooms because instructional leaders should know what is happening in these classrooms. Without the knowledge of what is taking place in the classroom, principals are also unable to appreciate and understand the problems teachers and students encounter.

Another factor for consideration for any instructional leader is that of *trust*. Trust is the cornerstone in the foundation for effective in-class supervision.[23] Trust is an absolute, and being in classrooms working with teachers will help build the trust that is the foundation necessary for leading teachers down the pathway to instructional improvement. It also gives instructional leaders the influence they must have if their intent is for teachers to listen and follow their leadership in guiding them to excellence.

As previously stated, there are several concerns teachers have that must not go unaddressed. In addition to the ten concerns previously mentioned, the following specifically relates to teacher and principal conferencing skills:

- to identify the teacher's interests and concerns in an appropriate manner (directive, informal, collaborative, or self-directed);
- to clarify the primary purpose of the observation is to improve teaching and learning;
- to reduce stress and make the teacher feel comfortable about the process; and
- to choose an observation tool and schedule the visit and post-conference.[24]

CONCLUDING THOUGHTS

Listing essential instructional leadership skills that leaders should use would be numerous, but listed below are four that are crucial for those working with teachers to improve instructional performance:

- Effective instructional leaders need to be resource providers.
- Effective instructional leaders need to be instructional resources.
- Effective instructional leaders need to be good communicators.
- Effective instructional leaders need to create a visible presence.[25]

For those individuals who choose to be an instructional leader, these skills must be learned—and more so, they must be practiced.

If principals are going to function as instructional leaders, it is time they recognize and begin to dedicate more time to what instructional leaders do.

Instructional leaders function differently in how they do what they do. This difference and focus must be on helping teachers get better at the essence of teaching: supporting and enhancing student achievement. If this does not become a priority, schools will significantly suffer the consequences, and neither teachers nor students will meet their full potential.

It must be asked if there is a problem that can be resolved to support better teaching and instructional leadership, and as this is further investigated, one can surmise that there is. Over the years, those in the field of education have seen that society is placing greater demands on teachers and teaching; therefore, it is paramount that educators are provided the preparation needed to help them improve instructional practices.

This starts with university preparation programs. These programs must make sure the information and training that is provided to potential teachers and school leaders prepares great teachers and instructional leaders who understand and know how to lead and how to support and improve instructional practices in the classroom.

This belief regarding instructional leadership preparation programs does not lack support. The course of study of many preparation programs for preparing instructional leaders does not always reflect a principal's real job and their support of teaching and learning.[26] This is truly sad because if principals cannot help teachers improve their instructional skills that support greater depths of student achievement, then how can there be great schools where teachers are effective instructors and students thrive in all aspects associated with learning?

It seems imperative that educators as a whole revisit what instructional leadership is all about, and that must start with those who are in positions of training these individuals. Revisiting instructional leadership requires us to redefine and refocus on the role of the principal as instructional leader and to remove multiple barriers that keep them from working with teachers to enhance and improve instruction. This training must focus on improving observations, assessing school culture and climate, addressing marginal teaching, and supporting adult learning.[27]

Another paramount issue that instructional leadership preparation programs must address are the leadership skills of those who are preparing others in their university classrooms to be instructional leaders in schools. Many of those at the university level who are charged with preparing them have never done what they are instructing those in their classes to do. This is truly a sad situation. It must be asked and addressed, How can anyone attempt to prepare others to do something they have never done themselves?

This adds greatly to the challenges and unanswered problems schools face today. It has already been stated that if universities fail to provide quality preparation for school leaders, they are failing schools and those who are attempting to lead them. University preparation programs must address this situation because if they expect the best from those they train for preparation, then universities must give their best preparation as well.

It must be understood that teachers can grow and get better and so can principals; if principals desire to be the instructional leaders they should be, they must do better. They must not fail in this capacity because without excellence in the classroom, children and teachers will suffer. This excellence must come from those who are in positions to lead and to help teachers get better at the essence of instruction. Principals must understand this because it starts with them.

NOTES

1. Whitaker, T. (2012). *What great principals do differently: 18 things that matter most*. Larchmont, NY: Eye on Education.

2. Zepeda, Sally J. (2017). *Instructional supervision: Applying tools and concepts* (4th ed.). New York, NY: Routledge.

3. McCann, T. M., Jones, A. C., & Aronoff, G. A. (2012). *Teaching matters most: A school leader's guide to improving classroom instruction*. Thousand Oaks, CA: Corwin Press.

4. Jones, J. R., & Henry, M. (2019, October). *Teachers perceptions and expectations of principals*. Paper presented at the meeting of the Southern Regional Council on Educational Administration, Fort Myers, FL.

5. Ibid.

6. Gall, M. D., & Acheson, K. A. (2010). *Clinical supervision and teacher development: Preservice and inservice applications* (6th ed.). New York, NY: Longman.

7. Fullan, M. (2008). *What's worth fighting for in the principalship*. New York, NY: Teachers College Press.

8. No Child Left Behind Act of 2001, P.L. 107–10, 20 U.S.C. § 6319 (2002). Retrieved from https://www2.ed.gov/nclb/overview/intro/execsumm.pdf.

9. Hoy, W. K., & Hoy, A. (2013). *Instructional leadership: A research-based guide to learning in Schools* (4th ed.). Boston, MA: Allyn and Bacon.

10. Sergiovanni, T. (2015). *The principalship: A reflective practice perspective* (7th ed.). New York, NY: Allyn and Bacon.

11. Zepeda, S. J. (2012). *The principal as instructional leader: A handbook for supervisors* (3rd ed.). New York, NY: Routledge.

12. Whitaker, T. (2012). *What great principals do differently: 18 things that matter most*. Larchmont, NY: Eye on Education.

13. Ubben, G. C., Hughes, L. W., & Norris, C. J. (2017). *The principal creative leadership for excellence in schools* (7th ed.). London, United Kingdom: Pearson.

14. Schmoker, M. (2016). *Results now: How we can achieve unprecedented improvements in teaching and learning*. Alexandria, VA: Association for Supervision and Curriculum Development.

15. Cotton, K. (2003). *Principals and Student Achievement: What the research says*. Alexandria, VA: ACSD Books.

16. Zepeda, S. J. (2012). *The principal as instructional leader*.

17. Parker, T., & Ziegler, C. (2005). Leading from the classroom. *Educational Leadership, 62,* (9), 47–51.

18. Sullivan, S., & Glanz, J. (2013). *Supervision that improves teaching: Strategies and Techniques* (4th ed.). Thousand Oaks, CA: Corwin Press.

19. Blase, J., & Blase, J. (2000). Effective instructional leadership: Teacher's perspectives on how principals promote teaching and learning in schools. *Journal of Educational Administration, 38* (2), 130–41. doi:10.1108/09578230010320082.

20. Fullan, M. (2015). *The new meaning of educational change* (4th ed.). New York, NY: Teachers College Press.

21. Bartoletti, J., & Connelly, G. (2013). *Leadership matters: What the research says about the importance of principal leadership*. Reston, VA: National Association of Secondary School Principals. Alexandria, VA: National Association of Elementary School Principals.

22. Jenkins, B. (2009). What it takes to be an instructional leader. *Principal, 88* (3), 34–39.

23. Nolan, J. F., & Hoover, L. A. (2011). *Teacher supervision and evaluation theory into practice* (3rd ed.). Hoboken, NJ: John Wiley and Sons.

24. Sullivan, S., & Glanz, J. (2013). *Supervision that improves teaching: Strategies and techniques* (4th ed.). Thousand Oaks, CA: Corwin Press.

25. Whitaker, B. (1997). Instructional leadership and principal visibility. *The Clearinghouse, 7,* (3), 155–56. doi:10.1080/00098655.1997.10543916.

26. Mendels, P. (Ed.). (2016). *Improving university principal preparation programs: Five themes from the field*. New York, NY: Wallace Foundation. Retrieved from https://www.wallacefoundation.org/knowledge-center/Documents/Improving-University-Principal-Preparation-Programs.pdf.

27. Zepeda, S. J. (2013). *The principal as instructional leader: A practical handbook* (3rd ed.). New York, NY: Routledge.

Chapter Three

Students' Assessment of Quality Teaching

This chapter addresses the second of the four dimensions for improving instructional practices, and that dimension is the student-to-teacher dimension. Ordinarily, principals are required to visit classrooms at least once or twice a year to observe and assess teaching and to provide feedback to teachers relative to that observation. Most would agree this one administrative function of observing and assessing teaching one or two times a year is not working very well and there is ample room for improvement.

These very infrequent observations do not provide sufficient information to the school leader who is observing the teacher if significant improvements need to be made. It can be asked, if school leaders do not spend sufficient time in classrooms observing teaching and assisting them in areas needing improvement, who does? Those who do spend sufficient time observing in the classrooms are students. Many would say students are not capable of measuring teaching performance, but most students do know how they learn and what teaching methods best support their specific learning needs.

Before discussion occurs relating to what students say about teaching and their learning, this chapter will first discuss what has occurred over the past several years that has caused the teaching profession to be where it currently is today. This requires the discussion of various legislative acts and policies that were supposed to address and improve teaching and learning. However, evidence suggests these numerous acts and policies in many ways did just the opposite. It must be understood: quality instruction and greater depths of student achievement simply cannot be legislatively mandated.

After a discussion of some of these various mandates, policies, and laws, it must be asked, if all these things are so good, then why change them every few years? The only possible answer to this educational dilemma is that their overall impact was not that effective, and it verifies one cannot mandate great teaching that improves and supports student academic achievement.

IT IS NOT ABOUT PROGRAMS OR MANDATES/LEGISLATION

In the past twenty-five to thirty years, all aspects associated with teaching and learning have changed, and more changes are inevitable as we continue into the twenty-first century. Changes happen so quickly that many schools simply cannot keep up with the multiplicity of them. Everyone outside of education seems to know how teachers should do what is called "educating children." Teachers continuously receive the brunt of criticism. Some even say teachers are said to be mediocre, illiterate, and completely incompetent.

In addition, good teachers are leaving the profession to find work in other professions. Even the prospective teachers are said to be drawn from the lower portion of the college population. If this is true, then educators must ask themselves if this could account for some of the reasons why students seem to be low achievers in the public schools.

Many of those who have gone through teacher preparation programs point out that the teacher education programs have been declared inadequate and ineffective.[1] They also say that in some in some cases, they are totally irrelevant, even detrimental to the careers of people going into the profession. This, coupled with people saying students are not learning, seems to provide a bleak picture of the teaching profession and student achievement; one might say that in many cases, it still looks very depressing.

Two questions that must be addressed regarding this are: Can there be excellence in the classroom without first-rate teachers? Can students master and apply course content to new learning? Educators can change the curriculum, buy more materials, change the physical environment, give more standardized exams (which will happen) and even lengthen the school day, but without quality teachers, all the change in the world will not produce the desired effect. The desired effect must promote greater depths of student achievement.

Many educators seem to be looking for that special program that will captivate students and arouse them to greater levels of academic achievement. It must be understood, there is no special program to replace the teacher, but helping them become better at instructional delivery must be the overall concern. As already stated, helping teachers improve instructional practices must be the primary concern for schools, and school leaders are responsible for this and must be held accountable for doing so.

It seems imperative that schools give teachers a chance to break away from their feelings of isolation and from the threat that so many mandates place on them. Teachers should be allowed to analyze their skills as they relate to the teaching process, and one primary way of doing this is to allow teachers to work with and observe each other. This also allows teachers to share with each other opinions and various teaching methods that can help all teachers, but especially those who feel isolated. This freedom from isolation will enhance instruction and also give students a better chance to master what is being taught to them.

The question that must be answered is, how do educators know when students have mastered course content and can apply it to further depths of learning that creates new learning? Surely, the results on high-stakes testing are not the answer to this question. Test scores cannot serve as the only basis for determining this. It seems safe to say that educators and policy makers want students to do well on these tests, but is that all they want? Today, schools are under tremendous pressure to improve student achievement, but most of the time, it is at the expense of failing to help teachers get better at instruction. However, as sad as it is, it seems that most of the emphasis is placed on the problem of lack of student achievement and not on its remedy.

It must be asked, where does all of this come from and why? The pressure that has been applied to schools today is driven from several sources. One could say it really got its start with *A Nation at Risk* (National Commission on Excellence in Education). This report centered on the need for greater accountability relating to student achievement. This report was based on the premise that schools were not meeting the needs of students if they were to compete in a global society.[2]

Therefore, politicians and policy makers suggested that schools needed to add more math and science to the curriculum, and at the same time, look at lengthening the school day. That itself is not that bad, but this was also coupled with increasing the requirements for high school graduation and developing rigorous assessments to evaluate student learning. Herein lies one of the sources of the problem.

Another report issued three years later, *A Nation Prepared: Teachers for the 21st Century* (Carnegie Corporation of New York), gave rise to additional discussions, and—this time—mostly regarding teachers and teaching. Even though this report talked about higher standards for students, it viewed teachers as the key component to school reform. It suggested if teachers were involved in curriculum development, instruction, and assessment, they would be able to implement the necessary components for greater student achievement.[3]

Teachers do need to be involved in the process of curriculum development, improvement of instructional skills and various forms of assessing student performance, but this is seldom done today. Ten years later, another report was issued that reinforced and focused on teaching. This could be called the "standards report" since it basically laid out a blueprint for higher standards for teacher licensure that included testing of teacher knowledge and a review of teacher preparation programs.[4] It has been continuous and again, in 2002, President Bush signed into law the *No Child Left Behind ACT (NCLB)*. This bill targeted federal resources to support state and local school improvements.[5]

It placed major importance on at-risk children with emphasis on K–3 reading instruction. It also placed greater importance on testing students, with states being required to establish proficiency levels. *NCLB* said that, beginning in 2002, new teachers in schools receiving funds under this law will meet certain standards, and by 2006, all teachers must meet these standards. All new teachers had to meet state certification requirements and/or pass state licensure examinations.

Another portion of the law required states to develop assessments aligned with state standards. Schools were held accountable for student progress. In retrospect, this progress has never occurred. Schools had to develop annual report cards demonstrating the degree of success for each student. Schools that did not show adequate progress over a two-year period would be identified by the state as needing corrective action. This correction could even lead to abolishment of the school. It is obvious those who mandated and implemented *NCLB* never understood how all of the implications were associated with great teaching and student learning.

This, again, is another classic example of individuals who are making decisions about what teachers and school leaders do but have never done it themselves. What makes this even more sad is that the legislatures making and passing these laws are receiving their ideas and recommendations regarding educational legislation from the Department of Education, and many of those individuals have never done what teachers and school leaders do on a daily basis.

One might think these mandates are calling for a new type of teacher and student. This may be true; however, the basic skills required for citizens are the same, but are they sufficient? Schools are being asked to prepare students who can demonstrate content mastery, knowledge, and skills. Through the education provided today for students, they should be able to test and apply ideas, look at concepts from many points of view, develop proficiency performances, inquire into a problem using a productive research strategy, produce a high-quality piece of work, understand the standards that indicate good performance, and be able to solve problems they have never encountered.[6]

This is needed today more than ever, but state and federal mandates are lacking in their ability to really address the issues associated with greater levels of student understanding and achievement. Many in the research community seem to be agreeing with this conceptual dimension for learning, and the type of instructional behaviors exhibited by teachers to promote this are needed. It might be easy to agree with this, but it must be asked, if schools do what is necessary to help teachers exhibit these instructional behaviors and more so, will the colleges of education enable new teachers to exhibit these behaviors?

It must be done! Again, let it be said, that students are worth educators' best efforts, and if they fail providing their best, they are failing their students. It is time policy makers and educators understand that student learning is based on construction of new knowledge, and students need to make sense of what they have learned—in a sense, reinvent it for themselves.[7] This will require students to be able to connect new learning to prior knowledge and be able to link what they learn in the curriculum to their own experiences and frames of reference.

Teachers must be able to guide students in a manner that will allow them to make these connections, but teachers must make these connections first and then demonstrate them in their classes through teaching how everything comes together and connects. Students are telling teachers they are unable to make these connections because everything seems to be structured on teaching content and then immediately testing students on what was taught. State and federal mandates have forgotten or, better yet, do not have any idea about how students learn.

The system and these mandates are failing students, and students are telling educators this, but no one seems be listening to them so they can do something to improve teacher performance that will better meet the specific needs of students. As previously mentioned, one crucial perspective—one that is seldom considered—is what students themselves say about teacher quality. Research in this area suggests that schools rarely listen to or even value what students say about teacher quality.

It is like going to see the doctor when one is sick, and the doctor asks him or her where it hurts, he or she tells the doctor where it hurts, and the doctor says, "You can't be hurting there." Even though research seems lacking in this area, some studies indicate that some schools do value what their students say about teaching effectiveness.

One school that allows its students to advise and even rate their teachers is George Mitchell School in London, England. Students in George Mitchell have been given *ownership* of their schooling. They observe and critique lessons, make suggestions to teachers regarding how they could improve their teaching, and they even interview perspective teachers. Classroom observations by students take place on a regular basis. Teachers take these student comments and adjust how they teach their lessons to how their students learn the content that is taught.

Listening to student's views on what they need from teachers seems to be the key that is missing today in the vast majority of most schools.[8] Changes made by teachers because of student comments have provided an overall growth in student achievement results. Currently, George Mitchell is one of the top schools in the country. All of this was accomplished without legislative mandates, and the cost was negligible—but results have been enormous.

This same thing can occur in most schools today if school leaders would work in consort with each other and allow students to share with them what they need from those teaching and leading schools. If teachers allow students to make the connections students say they need to make, that will require educators to change. More than that, policy makers must also learn that teaching and learning are much more than just delivering content and then testing to see where students rank by comparing them to other students around the country and world.

At the same time, colleges of education may need to break away from some of the practices they hold dear. If educators and policy makers keep doing what they have always done, the results will stay the same, and the profession of education will keep reaping the same results. This means educators and policy makers must stop searching for short-term solutions; that is, every quick fix that is available or appears on the market for sale.

It needs to be asked if the current Common Core addiction or other standards addictions represent more of the same—hopefully not, but if educators do not address improvements in the instructional process, more of the same results will continue. It is time educators and policy makers realize the problems in education (as difficult as they may be to solve) require long-term solutions, such as curriculum-focused professional development that leads to instructional improvement. This takes dynamic school leadership.

It is this type of school leadership that supports and promotes quality instruction that ushers in greater depths of student achievement—not programs or state and federal mandates. It must be understood, and it can be verified, that quality instruction is the heart of learning. Therefore, if instruction is the heart of learning, then how do educators know when or if quality instruction is taking place? Test scores cannot be the sole indicator. Teaching has been viewed from every possible way: from teachers who are professionally prepared by colleges of education to those who have been prepared through alternative routes.

It is not so much the route of preparation as it is the quality of the preparation. Is it so difficult for those who are preparing and working with educators to find the correct answers that would enable teachers to be better at instruction so students could achieve at higher levels? It could also be asked if students have the expertise to assess instruction that could help teachers get better. There is little research that does support that students do have the expertise to do this.

However, as previously stated, students do know for themselves what helps them learn. They may not know the pedagogical terminology, but they do know what they need from their teachers to help them be more successful in the classroom. Listening to what students say about teaching and their learning may seem a radical approach from the way most schools are structured, but if educators value learning, then it seems right they should listen to those who are the recipients of what is being taught.

WHAT STUDENTS ARE SAYING THEY NEED FROM TEACHERS

Teachers seldom ask students, who are their stakeholders, what they need from them to help them become successful at learning. As already noted, there is some research available that suggests students can assess instruction and can provide meaningful feedback to teachers relative to their learning needs.

One crucial perspective that is seldom considered is what students themselves say about teacher quality. Based on research that supports this, students do want their teachers to take time to listen to them.[9] Teaching effectiveness is dependent upon the interaction between the instructor's subject-matter knowledge and his or her teaching or pedagogical skills. Students believe their teachers should demonstrate clarity in their teaching and explanations of course content.[10] This seems to mean students who perceive better clarity from their teachers have a better opportunity for learning. Clarity is important and teachers must understand it might have a different meaning for each child.

Another major study supporting quality instruction occurred in Philadelphia when more than 250 students were interviewed over a three-year period. These students were in the eighth grade, representing six different schools. This study identified six distinct qualities students believed teachers should have that would enable them to achieve greater success in school. The qualities are:

- encourage students to complete assignments,
- maintain order in the classroom,

- offer students help when they need it,
- explain assignments and concepts,
- vary classroom activities,
- respect the students, and
- spend more time with the students on their learning activities.[11]

In addition, another major study—the largest study ever conducted about what students are saying they need from their teachers—has a tremendous amount of student comments to offer educators regarding what students say they need from teachers relating to teaching and learning. This study spanned a ten-year period in which over seventeen thousand students participated in assessing teaching performance that impacted their learning.

Listening to what students say about teaching and their learning may seem a radical approach from the way most schools are structured, but if educators value learning, then it seems right to say that educators should listen to those who are recipients of what is taught. This research seems significant for many reasons, as it is recent and gives educators seven valuable concerns listed by students. It seems appropriate that educators and policy makers should listen to these concerns and make efforts to see that improvements are made in these areas. This study provided evidence that students believed their teachers needed to:

- give them explanations they understand;
- teach them at a speed that is not too fast and not too slow;
- stay with a subject until the students understand it;
- in each lesson a teacher teaches, he or she should prepare students for the next lesson;
- allow students to talk about what they have learned;
- spend enough time on difficult subjects; and
- give students enough time for practice.[12]

It is noteworthy and must be understood by educators and policy makers that these seven effective teaching behaviors are observable, and it is the instructional leader's responsibility to ensure that teachers have assistance to improve in each area and any others in which teachers need help. Each of these behaviors suggested by students as well as what can be done to help teachers will be discussed in greater detail.

Give Them Explanations They Understand

Teachers must provide a roadmap for learning that students understand; once something is learned, it can then be used to facilitate new learning. This roadmap includes communicating goals, objectives, and expectations for the lesson. If students do not understand concepts being taught, then learning becomes almost impossible. For students to become engaged in learning, they must receive clear directions and explanations, and because teachers communicate with students mostly with language, that language must be audible and legible.[13] Therefore, it is imperative that teachers clearly communicate lessons that students can use to help them understand what the teacher is trying to teach.

Teach Them at a Speed That Is Not Too Fast and Not Too Slow

Students need feedback regarding what they have learned and concerning their progress. Teachers should use both oral and written feedback so students can monitor their own learning. This composite feedback will give students an opportunity to focus on what needs to be learned and possible steps they can take to help them learn. This feedback also provides students ownership of their own learning and will help them remain interested in learning. In many ways, this translates into pacing each lesson for all types of learners in classes.

For classrooms that are characterized by student engagement, pacing is appropriate for students and to the content to be learned, and suitable opportunities and time for closure should be provided. This gives students the time they need for learning, and they are not rushed in their work, nor does time "drag" while they are completing their work.[14] Students, in essence, are saying they need more time to absorb content if they are expected to apply it to new learning.

Stay with a Subject until the Students Understand It

One of the challenges that instructional leaders face is observing the lack of content in the lesson or the lack of organization used in teaching and in the materials. Most teachers perceive pressure to cover everything in the book or what state or school district officials say needs to be covered. A classic example of this is as follows: At the beginning of each school year, teachers are given dates and timelines they are to follow throughout the year. This timeline requires them to cover course content in a specified amount of time because in the spring of each year, students will be required to take high-stake tests that are supposed to measure content proficiency relative to certain courses.

This appears wrong, and students are telling educators it is wrong. But because of state and national mandates, teachers are required to press on even if students have not mastered course content. This practice represents another classic example of policy makers not understanding how students learn and that teachers need more time in addressing each student's learning needs. This leads to teaching content with insufficient depth and student understanding.

An attempt to cover too much material also leads to a lack of breadth of information, which promotes ineffective instruction. Many educators seem to be searching for an instructional model; one that has proven to be most effective—but is seldom used today—is available and it appears to demonstrate what students are saying regarding understanding of content. This model was developed by Madeline Hunter and indicates teachers should check for student understanding of content. This verification may require teachers to use various questioning techniques that allow students to explain in their own words what was learned and how they can apply it to new learning.[15]

This informal type of understanding content can be very effective and can support student understanding. Readers of this text are encouraged to look closely at this model and learn how to use it to support teaching and learning.

Each Lesson the Teachers Teach Should Prepare Students for the Next Lesson

It is essential that educators reach all students; therefore, teachers must use variable teaching methods to reach all learners. Teachers must know what types of learners are in their classrooms and adjust for each learner. Teachers must also realize what is taught should lead to something else to be learned. When this happens, students are learning content that should lead to new content to be learned.

The concept is not new and is even supported by the work of many of those who have developed evaluation models used in many schools today to assess teacher performance. These models stress that teachers must provide clear instructions and directions to what is to be taught. They further suggest that students should be able to facilitate their own understanding of what was taught and use it to promote further learning.[16] Based on what students are telling educators about their own learning needs; it is apparent this particular component of these various teacher evaluation models is being inadequately assessed by school leaders.

Allow Students to Talk about What They Have Learned

Students are asking for and need time to discuss what they have been taught so they can learn from each other and apply what was taught to how they learn. Teachers must allocate time for student learning and give them time to discuss issues they may need clarified. It is also suggested that teachers should allow students to compile the information taught and process it in the way they learn.[17] In addition, teachers should provide continuous and frequent opportunities for students to express their thoughts.[18]

Discussion time should provide students a chance to develop skills of listening, speaking, and participating as members of a group. It seems imperative that maximum student participation should be sought by all teachers.

Spend Enough Time on Difficult Subjects

Teachers must be given sufficient time to spend on subjects that are difficult for students and not be pressured to cover content at the expense of students not learning it. Content covered does not always mean content learned. Students must be given time to process what has been taught because it is a major factor in what they learn and remember. It is interesting to note, almost every study examining time and learning has found a significant relationship between time spent on content relates either positively or negatively to student learning.[19]

Teachers should seek resources that support teaching and learning, though that does not necessarily mean financial resources. One appropriate (but often overlooked) resource teachers can use is each other. Instructional leaders should guarantee teachers have time to observe each other's classes collaboratively and have time to discuss what they observed and what possible modifications to the improvement of instruction can be made.

Give Students Enough Time for Practice

As previously stated, the current system tends to force teachers to cover breadth and not depth. Students are asking teachers to slow down to give them time to learn so they can apply what is being taught. It is the depth of content students need to learn that can help them add the breadth for learning desired of them. Research in this area identifies six teaching functions that are based on effective instruction. They are:

- review, checking previous day's work (and reteaching if necessary)
- presenting new content/skills
- initial student practice (and checking for understanding)

TEXTBOX 3.1. MY TEACHER CHECKLIST

Jones/Henry—What I Need from My Teacher

Students, I want to be the best teacher I can be. For me to be able to do that, I need feedback from you. Below is a checklist that will help me see what I am doing that is helpful to you and what I need to improve. Be honest.

Instructions: Place an *X* on the line under the category that, in your opinion, best describes each statement. Do not write your name on this paper.

		2	1	0
		All of the time	Some of the time	Never
1.	You give explanations we understand.	____	____	____
2.	You teach us at a speed that is not too fast and not too slow.	____	____	____
3.	You stay with a subject until we understand it.	____	____	____
4.	You teach things step-by-step.	____	____	____
5.	You explain a subject and then give us time to ask questions.	____	____	____
6.	In each lesson you teach, you prepare us for the next lesson.	____	____	____
7.	You allow us to talk about what we have learned.	____	____	____
8.	You ask if we know what to do and how to do it.	____	____	____
9.	You show us how to do our class work.	____	____	____
10.	You explain an assignment and how to complete it.	____	____	____
11.	You spend enough time on difficult subjects.	____	____	____
12.	You show and explain how to do our homework.	____	____	____
13.	You give us enough time for practice.	____	____	____
14.	You answer our questions.	____	____	____
15.	You help us understand what we have learned and why it is important.	____	____	____

Comments: (Write anything you want to add) _____
_____
_____

- feedback and correctives (and reteaching if necessary)
- student independent practice
- weekly and monthly reviews

It is apparent the main focus associated with teaching must be to help students learn by teachers imparting knowledge to them and by creating situations that foster and allow students to learn and apply what has been taught to them. One function relates specifically to guided practice, and this suggests that students need teachers to give greater time for practice, especially as it applies to misunderstandings or possible misconceptions.[20] To find out what students are saying about their individual learning needs as they relate to assisting teachers in providing the instruction that supports those learning needs, the questionnaire in textbox 3.1 can be tremendously beneficial if students are afforded the opportunity to complete it.

CONCLUDING THOUGHTS

Teachers and school leaders must seriously consider what students are telling them they need from them to enhance their learning, and school instructional leaders must make significant changes in the ways they view teaching and assist teachers in improving their instructional skills. If students are worth educators' best efforts, then maybe it is time the educational profession review what is already known about improving instructional practices and return to the basics of it. In efforts to improve instructional practices, there have been all types of schemes and devices used to address instructional improvement.

Most of these schemes and devices have again been mandated by policy makers and (it has already been said) most of these policy makers have never taught a day in their lives. But by passing these mandates, they seem to be saying they know what students need from their teachers and what needs to be done to improve instruction. This speaks specifically to the way school leaders work with teachers regarding instructional improvement. This also relates to the supervisory practices used by school leaders to assess instruction. Again, these practices are usually mandated by policy makers.

If educators and policy makers are truly interested in meeting the educational needs of every student in schools, significant changes must take place. These changes are paramount and will require policy makers and school and district leaders to get serious about this as well. One of the best ways to improve instructional practices that meet the needs of every student is for school leaders to change the way they work with teachers to improve instruction. This means supervisory practices will need to change.

One of the most persistent problems in supervision of instruction today is the dilemma between (*a*) evaluating a teacher to make decisions about retention, promotion, and tenure; and (*b*) working with the teacher as a friendly critic or colleague to help develop instructional skills teachers want to use and to expand the repertoire of strategies that can be employed.[21] Working with teachers as a friendly critic is enlightening, and this concept needs to be examined fully. School leaders must consider the use of more formative types of assessing instruction. This includes listening to what students say they need from their teachers to assist their learning needs.

Formative assessment can be defined as assessment that encourages a process of reflective practice; engaging in formative assessment supports rapid feedback. This feedback can also be derived from students, but in most cases, it is not used at all. Student's views and opinions represent a great way to formatively view and assess instruction. Formative types of assessment give students, teachers, and school leaders a chance to have open dialogue about what and how aspects have been taught. This is what students are desiring to do and it can be a huge benefit for all educators.

Formative assessment is continuous and offers feedback, and gives the leader and teacher time to gather information to discuss progress toward goals and to get a clearer picture of the types of professional learning opportunities that would be helpful based on performance.[22] This would also allow instructional leaders and teachers to identify and better understand strengths and weaknesses and ways to determine how to grow. Simply defined: this is what all students deserve.

In addition, formative assessment is a function intended to assist and support teachers in professional growth and the improvement of teaching that our students deserve and are asking for from every educator.[23] Instructional leaders should desire this as well and work with teachers to improve their instructional skills and help them in ways that create positive conversations about what needs to be done to enhance the teaching process. This would also require principals to function as instructional leaders and be in classrooms more by observing and working as a friendly critic who supports teaching and learning.

But the question must be asked, is this something that is truly desired, and if so, why is collegiality not supported and teachers encouraged to work cooperatively with each other to address these issues known to enhance instructional practices? This process is not mandated by policy makers, so why should educators use something that is not required of them? The answer to this is simple.

If educators and policy makers desire to improve the essence of teaching that enhances student learning and what students are telling us they need from teachers that supports this learning, it is a professional responsibility and obligation to enact research-based supports and practices proven to be effective. This also means policy makers will need to review mandates and make sure they are aligned with these practices that have been proven to work. Students and teachers need to have a voice in this process and this need must be understood by policy makers.

Simply put, if instruction is the heart of learning, it is, therefore, an obligation to do all that can be done to improve it because students are entitled to educators' best efforts. Anything less than their best is an absolute failure for students.

NOTES

1. Zumwalt, K. (1986). Introduction. In K. K. Zumwalt (Ed.), *Improving teaching ASCD yearbook* (pp. vii–x). Alexandria, VA: Association for Supervision and Curriculum Development.

2. National Commission on Excellence in Education. (1983). *A nation at risk: The imperative for educational reform.* Washington, DC: U.S. Government Printing Office.

3. Carnegie Corporation of New York. (1986). *A nation prepared: Teachers for the 21st century.* New York.

4. National Commission on Teaching and America's Future. (1996). *What matters most: Teaching and America's future.* New York: Teachers College Press.

5. No Child Left Behind Act of 2001 107th Congress (2001–2002). Retrieved fromhttps://www.congress.gov/bill/107th-congress/house-bill/1#:~:text=No%20 Child%20Left%20Behind%20Act%20of%202001%20%2D%20Amends%20the% 20Elementary,reauthorize%2C%20and%20consolidate%20various%20programs.

6. Darling-Hammond, L. (1997). *The right to learn: A blueprint for creating schools that work.* San Francisco, CA: Jossey-Bass.

7. Liberman, A., & Miller, L. (2000). Teaching and teacher development: A new synthesis for a new century. In R. S. Brandt (Ed.), *Education in a new era* (pp. 47–66). Alexandria, VA: Association for Supervision and Curriculum Development.

8. Wilce, H. (2006). The school where pupils rate their teachers, *The Independent Online Edition, 16,* 1–3. Retrieved from http://www.education.independent.co.uk/ schools.article345645.ece.

9. Sabine, G. A. (1971). *How students rate their schools and teachers.* Washington, DC: NASSP. Retrieved from http://www.education.independent.co.uk/schools .article345645.ece.

10. Walls, R. T. (1999). Stack the deck in favor of your students by using the four aces for effective teaching. *The Journal of Effective Teaching, 5* (2), 1–7. Retrieved from https://www.scribd.com/document/14003103/Four-Aces-of-Effective -Teaching.

11. Wilson, B., & Corbett, D. (2014). *Listening to urban kids: School reform and the teachers they want.* Albany, NY: SUNY Press.

12. Jones, J., & Henry, M. (2019). Students' Assessment of Teacher Quality: Recommendations for Improvement. *Southeast Journal of Educational Administration, 19* (3), 1–16.

13. Danielson, C. (2007). *Enhancing professional practice: A framework for teaching* (2nd ed.). Alexandria, VA: ASCD Publications.

14. Ibid.

15. Hunter, M. (1991). *The Madeline Hunter Model of Mastery Learning.* Retrieved December 15, 2020 from https://www.csun.edu/sites/default/files/Holle-Lesson-Planning.pdf.

16. Marzano, R. J. (2017). *The new art and science of teaching.* Bloomington, IL: Solution Tree.

17. Wong, H. K., & Wong, R. (1998). *The first day of school.* Mountain View, CA: Harry K. Wong Publications.

18. Oliva, P. F., & Pawlas, G. E. (1998). *Supervision for today's schools* (5th ed.). White Plains, NY: Longman.

19. Berliner, D. (1988). Simple views of effective teaching and simple theory of classroom instruction. In D. Berliner & B. Rosenshine (Eds.), *Talks to teachers* (pp. 93–110). New York, NY: Random House.

20. Rosenshine, B., & Stevens, R. (1986). *Second handbook of research on teaching.* Chicago, IL: Rand McNally.

21. Acheson, K. A., & Gall, M. D. (2003). *Clinical supervision and teacher development* (5th ed.). New York, NY: John Wiley and Sons.

22. Zepeda, S. J. (2017). *Instructional supervision: Applying tools and concepts* (4th ed.). New York, NY: Routledge.

23. Glickman, C. D., Gordon, S. P., & Ross-Gordon, J. M. (2014). *Supervision and instructional Leadership: A developmental approach* (9th ed.). Boston, MA: Pearson.

Chapter Four

Is There an Instructional Leader in the School?

The question that must be asked is what gives anyone the right to be an instructional leader in a school today? It certainly is not gained by election or appointment. Neither does having a position, title, rank, or degrees qualify anyone to be a leader of a school. The ability to lead a school cannot be conferred and does not come automatically from age or experience. It would be accurate to say that no one can be given the right to lead. The right to lead can only be earned, and it must be understood by those desiring to do so that it takes time and dedication from those who desire to lead.

Today, more than ever, the practice of instructional leadership has such an urgent need to help teachers excel in the classroom by becoming dynamic teachers. Many challenges associated with leading the school might cause problems that can force the school leader to get off course occasionally, but getting back on track as the leader of leaders is a must. When addressing this, it must be recognized and understood that challenges in today's schools are increasing in frequency, complexity, and intensity, influencing a demand for a new level of leadership excellence from school leaders.[1]

It is essential, especially for those who consider themselves to be instructional leaders, to focus on helping teachers improve the essence of instruction. If the desire is to see children in schools excel to greater depths of learning, then principals as instructional leaders must work with teachers to improve all aspects related to what is taking place in the classroom.

Teaching cannot be reduced to a prescription or formula that applies to every teacher. It is the primary function of the instructional leader to analyze teaching and to possess the skills necessary to work with every teacher to help them improve instructionally. This will not become a reality if the one functioning as the instructional leader is not in classrooms supporting and working with teachers. As was previously stated in chapter one and throughout this book, if schools expect greater student academic achievement, this greatly depends on the leaders within the schools and the conditions they *must* create to ensure that professional growth and teaching expertise are maximized.

Good teaching is a must in schools today, and good teaching results when there is a match between strategies, content, students, and the teacher. At the same time, teachers must not only draw upon what is known about the teaching-learning process from research but they must also orchestrate all the variables within the classroom to produce maximum learning for all students.[2] The instructional leader must understand this and be able to assist teachers in orchestrating these variables.

As the instructional leader, it is also imperative to be aware of instructional problems that teachers face. If the desire is to see children in our schools excel to greater depths of learning, then principals as instructional leaders must work with teachers to improve all aspects related to teaching. The desire must be to improve the teaching and learning process. It is a professional responsibility to do those things that research supports and practice has proven to be effective.

This chapter will focus on practical skills and strategies instructional leaders can use when hiring and working with teachers to enhance instructional practices. Instruction is the heart of learning; therefore, all instructional leaders have an obligation and responsibility to do all they can to improve it. Educators must realize all students in schools are entitled to their best efforts in all that educators can do and provide for them. Students cannot be given anything less than their best. If educators are not providing the best, they are leading and directing them in a misguided fashion that leads students down a pathway to nowhere.

It seems apparent in some schools today that all educators do not fully understand what the two main responsibilities of schools should be. It simply comes down to two words, *teaching* and *learning*. If these two things are not fully understood, then schools usually find themselves in serious trouble. Understanding these functions requires more than lip service. It requires everyone in the school to be intentional about how they are to support teaching and learning, and it must start with those who are responsible for leading schools.

This means the school leader's primary focus and function must be in these two areas, but the first focus must be on teaching—after that comes the learning focus. It is apparent that in high achieving schools, instructional leaders emphasize instruction as the most important goal of the school, and it should lead to better learning.[3] This also requires leaders of schools to be intentional about why they do what they do, and leading intentionally will be discussed more and in greater depth later in this chapter.

Being intentional will at times cause school leaders to feel as if they are always climbing a hill and always wondering if they will ever reach the top. Practicing leadership intentionally at times will cause the leader to perceive that everything worthwhile is uphill.[4] This definitely applies to those leading schools today and seeking to improve them. It is also fair to say that what is done in schools that relates to teaching and learning is definitely worthwhile. This also means that striving for excellence at times may seem very hard, but the only way it is impossible to achieve is to not attempt it.

The major task school leaders have is to lead teachers to excellence of instruction and this requires being intentional and calculating every move that is made regarding this. Also, every move must have purpose that leads to meaning. Every time the leader is in a classroom or communicating with teachers and students about teaching and learning, it must be continuously reinforced with a purpose that supports it. At the same time, it must be learned and fully understood that hiring, developing, and retaining the best faculty takes strategy and an enormous amount of preparation and time to be dedicated to this process.

PREPARING FOR SELECTION OF SCHOOL PERSONNEL: HIRE THE RIGHT PEOPLE

There is no question that the number one influence on the quality of schools and the instruction they provide starts first with the instructional leader and then carries over into the quality of excellence found in those teaching students within the school. It takes this combination of excellence to make the school outstanding. The desire for excellence places a huge burden on the instructional leader regarding who is currently in the classroom and those who need to be hired to be in the classrooms.

It is safe to say that recruitment is not so much about the number of applicants as it is about the quality of applicants who match the criteria needed to fill teaching and staff vacancies. It is important to reconcile why recruitment is necessary; therefore, the concern is not whether schools can fill a position or how to fill it, but rather to do it well. There are three compelling criteria that should be understood by instructional leaders and followed when recruiting and hiring school personnel:

- Those hiring should learn to make distinctions in what separates applicants.
- Great schools get better by having the best teachers and staff.
- Those hiring shouldn't just fill positions but hire the best to fill the positions.

For teaching vacancies, it must be understood that the teaching will only be as good as the person doing the teaching, and selecting the wrong teacher not only costs monetarily but also costs in lost learning and effectiveness for students. Therefore, school leaders must be intentional about the hiring process. It is imperative for school leaders to understand those closest to them will make or break them, and those closest to them are teachers.

Selection of Interviewing Team

Using a team consisting of staff and teachers is the best approach when reviewing potential applicants for positions in the school. The team members must also match the needs for the various positions under consideration. Instructional leaders should be on the screening/interviewing team, and at the same time, it is not enough to simply select the best people to serve on the interview team—they also need to be trained on interviewing.

Selecting Teachers and Staff

As demographic and curriculum changes influence the direction of the educational system, selection of the best teachers and staff should become more specific and more critical since, in most cases, they will be the ones who will be responding to the demographic needs of children and the curricular changes of the school. It is the responsibility of the school leader to match candidates to positions and the needs of the school. This includes the characteristics, education, diversity, and experiences of applicants, and it is much harder to do with teacher shortages (but that does not mean leaders should stop seeking the best teachers to fill their vacancies).

It is extremely important to make sure those on the hiring team can make distinctions between applicants. As the team performs their duties of reviewing, interviewing, and—finally—recommending someone to hire, they should always remember to hire up and to keep in mind there is something much more important and scarcer than ability; that is, their ability to recognize quality and talent when they see it. If the team selects well, the benefits are multiplied and, likewise, if they select poorly the problems can potentially be multiplied in the opposite direction.

It is important to know that before the school hires any new teacher or staff member, the options are nearly limitless, but once the hiring decision is made, options are few. The team must see the bigger picture, and that picture relates specifically to what students' needs are in the school. Individual schools have different needs; therefore, the team must know exactly what those needs are.

One thing the school leader and team can develop is an inventory of needs, and it could look similar to the following list of an assessment of needs.

- What is the assessment of needs for the school?
- What assets are currently on hand?
- What are the abilities of the applicants?
- What are the attitudes like for the applicants?
- What are the accomplishments of the applicants?

Understanding the application of this assessment of needs is extremely important, but it is equally important to know if an exceptional individual is available but doesn't necessarily match the current needs. The leader and team should consider an individual who might be in this category and do whatever they can do to possibly hire that person because, in the long run, that individual will add value and have a positive impact on the school.

After the interview team has been established, it is now time for the face-to-face interview. It is extremely important to make sure all of those being interviewed are asked the same questions. It is also important to make sure all questions asked require those being interviewed to discuss their teaching skills and how those skills have proven to have a positive impact on student learning.

There are several questions the committee can ask of teacher applicants, but the following eight questions require them to address and discuss what quality instruction looks like and the potential results that follow it:

- What intrigues you about teaching in this school?
- How do you define your teaching style and the steps you take to reach every student in your classroom?
- How do your teaching style and these steps you previously shared with us collectively engage students?
- How would you define your teaching strengths, and how do they foster better teaching and learning?
- If one of the search committee members came into your classroom, what would you hope they would see?
- What do you believe students' expectations are of their teachers?
- Can you give examples of ways you interact with parents?

This process of hiring must be supported with great intentions; that is, support hiring great people and then supporting them. It is very important to hire great people and those a leader inherits, help them become great.[5] Without the understanding and application of what this means, schools will not flourish.

Any great instructional leader will always be seeking ways to assist teachers in areas that improve and support teaching and learning.

This means school leaders must be great teachers themselves and have the awareness of this being a priority, continuously striving to perfect their own teaching skills. How else can they help teachers improve their instructional skills, if they are not a great teacher themselves? Instructional leaders should always be seeking ways to constantly work with their teachers for improvement purposes.

Doing this means the school leader places value in quality instruction that supports hiring and maintaining outstanding faculty. They also must be capable of developing teachers into teams of leaders who can work with each other in developing leaders among themselves—leaders who deliver quality instruction to every student in the school. Once the school has selected the best people to fill the various positions, it is time for those leading to begin to lead intentionally.

LEADING INTENTIONALLY

The question must be asked, How do instructional leaders lead intentionally? It is extremely important to understand what it means to be an intentional school leader. Many believe it is the same as functioning in an assertive or very decisive manner. This is definitely not the case, but it must be understood there will be times when a school leader's decisions may seem assertive—depending on the situation or potential dilemma they may find themselves in at a given time.

Intentional leadership requires school leaders to make it a core value in their leading abilities and to continually stay focused on these values. Teachers, students, and community members will always see the instructional leaders who lead intentionally as deliberate and caring individuals. Their plans are clearly understood as well as focused on positive results that enable everyone in the school to never question their purposes and the directions in which they are leading the school.

Instructional leaders must learn to intentionally put practices into place in their schools that support this; there are five of these practices that can be used by instructional leaders to assist them in guiding and leading teachers, staff, and students to excellence. The five steps for intentional leadership practices are:

- place value in building relationships,
- place value in quality teaching,

- place value in being in classrooms,
- place value in helping students learn, and
- place value in teachers, staff, and students.

Place Value in Building Relationships

The key to working with teachers effectively is in the relationships the instructional leader builds with each teacher in the school. For accentuation purposes, the most important way to develop relationships comes from being accessible to teachers and by being in classrooms helping teachers with their instructional needs. After these relationships have been developed, it gives the instructional leader the trust from their teachers that is absolutely essential in having the influence to lead and guide them to multiple areas of improvement.

This can be accomplished in many ways, but the school leader should constantly be thinking of ways to add value to every aspect of their teachers' professional lives. It is important to understand what drives them and what they are passionate about, even when they are out of the school.

Place Value in Quality Teaching

Valuing teaching will never be done unless the school leader is in classrooms, assisting teachers to excellence. Once this is understood and implemented, it should be demonstrated daily. Quality teaching must be incorporated in every classroom; when the instructional leader is working with teachers in the classroom, it places value on what the teacher is doing. Another example of valuing teaching is through formal and informal discussions with teachers.

In many cases, the formal discussions only occur when the teacher needs direct assistance on teaching performance or possibly during a conference that might relate to dismissal. Informal discussions are more important and should be done daily. A great example of an informal discussion could be as simple as the instructional leader walking down the hallway of the school and overhearing a teacher discussing course content with their students.

Later that day (or possibly the next day), the school leader should find some personal time to tell the teacher how impressed they were with the teaching they overheard while walking in the hallway. This adds value to what teachers are doing and also continues to build relationships that are crucial for the effective leadership that supports better instruction. Building these relationships with teachers also demonstrate and reinforces to them how valuable it is for them to develop positive relationships with their students.

Place Value in Being in Classrooms

As has been stated numerous times, the most important thing school leaders can do is to be in classrooms supporting and working with teachers to improve the essence of instruction. Again, this should not be the "one-or-two-times-per-year visit" that many consider sufficient. It should be a continuous intentional process, and once it becomes this, it demonstrates caring and dedication to what teachers do—that is, teaching.

In addition, it shows students the instructional leader cares about them and their needs. It also signals to teachers and students the instructional leader supports teachers and teaching. Not being in classrooms signals that teaching and student learning are devalued and leaves teachers and students in a state of being alone and isolated.

Place Value in Helping Students Learn

As has been said numerous times, one of the primary functions of a school is to increase greater depths of student learning. This does not and cannot take place in a vacuum. School leaders and teachers must be highly engaged in the teaching/learning process. This takes time and a complete understanding of what each student's needs are if schools are going to assist them as well as provide better support for their learning and accessing opportunities available to them. Learning is necessary for every student, and that requires educators to frame learning as the number one criterion in schools.

Instructional leaders and teachers must never forget that learning is not just what they teach in their classrooms. It must be understood, emphasized, and cultivated in students that it is a lifelong commitment. Transmitting this as a value to students can impact their lives through adulthood. Additionally, instructional leaders must see that teachers understand, emphasize, and engage students in learning and understand that living a life without learning is nonnegotiable.

Place Value in Teachers, Staff, and Students

Instructional leaders should continuously be looking for ways to add value to their teachers', staff's, and students' lives. It is important to understand what drives them and what they are passionate about in their school and home lives. Doing this will help them realize the instructional leader places great priority on them outside of the schoolhouse and will also make them feel their role in the leader's life has purpose and meaning.

This will benefit the overall teaching and learning process in many ways. Doing this gives teachers, staff, and students a gift of purpose, and with this gift of purpose in their lives, everyone will perform better. This is what is needed in schools today, but the instructional leader must look at this with an intentional mindset and make it part of what they do daily.

All of this seems pretty simple, and it must be understood when instructional leaders add value to their students and teachers, they add value to the school and what it is trying to accomplish. Adding this value in teachers and students will assist instructional leaders in adding value to everything they try to do as the schools strive to excellence. This, in turn, will pay huge dividends to the school as a whole by teaching and leading others how to add value to their lives.

Instructional leaders must always work on themselves when it comes to leading intentionally. The preparation it takes for each day requires advanced thinking from the leader, who must clearly understand the rationale for this and clearly recognize that it first starts with those leading the school. Once the school leader begins to follow the five steps for intentional leadership and practices them daily, great results will begin to happen in multiple ways. They will also add value for themselves, but more so for the teachers, staff, and students they are attempting to lead.

Following these steps will allow the school leader to see they are not only bringing purpose to the daily routines of the school but also to every person inside the school. This will assist the school leader in generating buy in for those things the school places value in, and more teachers, staff, and students will also see the value in what can be done and accomplished. This alone will have a positive impact on the school and what it is attempting to achieve.

The negative aspects associated with school leaders not leading from an intentional perspective can cause a lack of respect because they can slow down the direction the school should be taking—and they can waste everyone's time. This waste of time is usually translated into discouragement from teachers, staff, and students, who are trying to follow the directions of the school leader. This also translates into teachers losing their momentum in the classroom and students will eventually suffer from this loss of momentum.

Therefore, the school leader must demonstrate and make leading intentionally a daily habit—not one that is just practiced inadvertently—because habits will make school leaders what they really are. If leading intentionally is what the school leader's intent is, it then requires them to ask themselves some thought-provoking questions:

- What do I need to improve?
- What prevents me from being more intentional in my leadership skills?
- What personal habits need to change in my life?
- How can I be more accountable to those I am leading?

WHAT DO I NEED TO IMPROVE?

Every person in any school leadership position can always improve in many facets related to their leading skills and abilities. This means there are always areas for improvement and, again, improvement must start with those who are leading. It must start on the inside and then move to the outside. For example, one area of improvement can occur when school leaders have faculty meetings with their teachers. Teachers should never leave faculty meetings unsure of what was said or what they should do about a certain situation they may be dealing with in their classrooms.

Leading intentionally requires instructional leaders to clearly define their desire for their teachers to express themselves and not to feel restrained when doing so. It is imperative to seek any potential recommendations from those school leaders who are attempting to lead, and these meetings are a great place to seek advice that can allow for leadership improvement.

What Prevents Me from Being More Intentional in My Leadership Skills?

To fully understand what prevents school leaders from being more intentional, it is critical for them to create agendas for the school with others and to make sure high expectations are set for everyone. These expectations must be fully explained, understood, and accepted from teachers who are following the school leader. This will create a healthy environment where everyone feels welcome and wants to participate effectively in what the school does to increase teacher and student productivity in the classroom.

Many school leaders may fail in leading intentionally because they feel pressed for time to accomplish things that are necessary. It is essential that school leaders stay focused on what matters most: great teaching. There will be times when things will arise that need the school leader's urgent attention. That is understandable, but this cannot be the norm. Again, their major focus must be on teaching, learning, and intentionally working with teachers to improve their teaching performance.

What Personal Habits Need to Change in My Life?

As previously stated, habits tend to make leaders what they are. Everyone has some bad habits, and great school leaders cannot afford to make decisions from those bad habits. Their intention must be to lead and lead well. Therefore, the first habit that school leaders must address pertains to how they reflect on decisions they make and the language they use in discussions with teachers, students, and those outside the school. Before school leaders address an important issue, they must intentionally dedicate time for clarifying and thinking about what they may say when they express their viewpoint about something important to the operation of the school.

Very seldom, if ever, should it be only the leader's way of doing things; however, that appears to be the reality in many schools today, and that needs to change. Great school leaders understand that buy in comes when everyone is involved in clarifying issues that allow the school to better address the concerns that are most important and have an impact on everyone in the school.

The second habit that needs to be addressed is when school leaders allow their feelings to rule their leading, especially when things are getting done in a timely manner. This situation occurs in every school, and getting upset to the point where everyone in the school sees the leader's discontentment will cause great concern from those trying to follow the leader. This can cause great discord and relational problems in the school. In addition, this can cause anger and discouragement from everyone in the school, and teachers will usually take these situations into the classroom, which is something that should not be taken there.

How Can I Be More Accountable to Those I Am Leading?

There is nothing that can destroy a school more than teachers and staff not understanding what they are to do after meeting with the instructional leader about a situation that needs clarification. Once the meeting is taking place, teachers and staff should be there, not drifting in and out of the room. This builds a culture that is intentional about getting things accomplished for the good of the school, and it holds everyone accountable to each other for accomplishing goals that might need clarification.

Instructional leaders who do not understand intentional leadership and how to make it a daily activity in their own leadership lives will not comprehend what can be done to improve the overall effectiveness of the school and the value of the school's human capital. Recognizing and following these five steps for intentional leadership, as discussed in this chapter, will also enable the school leader to be able to demonstrate and, most importantly, to understand that all teachers in schools should be recognized as leaders.

This is greatly supported by the Wallace Report, stating that principals today must be instructional leaders capable of developing a team of leaders who deliver effective instruction to every student.[6] Treating everyone as leaders helps provide encouragement that provides support for better teaching and learning.

CONCLUDING THOUGHTS

In schools today, it appears no one is holding anyone accountable to what instructional leaders should be doing as it relates to improving all aspects associated with the improvement of instruction. They must be held accountable to those they are attempting to lead and to the students who are in their schools. They must also remember they are accountable to themselves and if they understand this, they will become the leader their school needs.

This accountability must be intentional; it starts with self and is passed to others in the school through the actions the leader takes with themselves first. In the last thirty years, this self-accountability seems to have disappeared, and, in many cases, blaming a predecessor or working conditions seems to be the norm. Blame is easy to place on someone else, but the truly great instructional leaders lay the blame at their feet.

If the leader is new to the school, blame should not be placed at the feet of others for the conditions they may have inherited when their turn comes to lead the school. When leading people in the school, the leader is charged to repair, replenish, and rebuild what might be broken and not to place blame on others. Placing blame on others never solves the problem or rebuilds the school. The job of the instructional leader is to make the school great, not to dwell on things that someone else caused to be broken.

As an instructional leader of a school, it is wise to remember that everyone in and outside of the school is watching and listening to every statement and action that comes from the school. Others are watching every step the instructional leader takes. It is imperative to build a reputation of integrity, honesty, and character in every decision that is made regarding the school.

However, from time to time, all school leaders find themselves dealing with tough situations, and as they come upon them, they must begin to develop a strategy or plan to deal with every one of them. Once this technique and skill is learned, the leader can then begin to act intentionally about how to handle these situations. This requires the school leader to be deliberate and thoughtful about what their next step should be. The end result is what is being sought, and the results may have a huge impact on the school and what the school is trying to accomplish.

It is probably safe to say that all instructional leaders do want to surround themselves with great teachers. They know that great teaching is what students need to help them become more successful in all aspects of their lives. Great instructional leaders also know that *fixed people fix people.* This means working to improve the front end will help create better results on the back end of things. Equating this to education means better teaching, equaling greater depths of student learning.

When leading intentionally, it requires moving with predetermined goals and objectives and with purpose. Every act and every move that the school leader makes should have purpose that leads to meaning and understanding for everyone in the school. Instructional leaders must understand that creating a great faculty takes strategy of thought and great preparation that must be supported with great intentions to accomplish this.

It must be understood, the key to becoming an effective instructional leader is not to focus on making other people follow, but on making oneself the kind of person others want to follow. He or she must become the leader whom others can trust to take them where they need to go. When the leader is intentional, he or she chooses to make decisions and take action on what is really important to the school. Being intentional means being clear up front about what can be achieved when teachers, staff, and students are involved in making everything better in the school.

At various times during the leadership journey, instructional leaders can find themselves in isolation just as teachers do, but as they evaluate the actions they have taken and have observed the positive changes resulting from the intentional leadership they have utilized, they will see a great change in the school and that significant positive improvements have been made. Intentional leading helps the instructional leader of the school set a course for the school rather than leading by aimlessly wandering around and getting nowhere. It gives the school leader the freedom to make time for the things that are truly important and sets the stage for the school to become a family, able to accomplish great things together.

This also gives them time to build a culture that supports growth that is transformative. In that regard, it could be suggested that principals who are attempting to develop as effective instructional leaders should work to integrate reflection and growth to build a school culture of individuals with shared and critical examination for instructional improvement.[7] Again, the leader must be intentional in these endeavors.

Instructional leaders must prepare every day in advance by thinking of ways they can go out of their way in leading their schools intentionally as opposed to the reactionary mindset so many seem to have. This represents an investment that will provide great returns to the leader and the school. Once the leader begins the process of developing and building up his or her teachers, staff, and students in the school, this will assist him or her by giving everyday purpose to all the things that have value in the school.

This indicates an investment that will provide great returns to the leader, teachers, staff, and students. Once the leader begins this developmental process and it adds value to what they are doing, then more people will be creating value, which is very powerful. When the leader begins the process of thinking about the magnitude of how others' lives can be changed by such a small step, it makes everyone in the school better.

NOTES

1. Green R. L. (2005). *Practicing the art of leadership* (2nd ed.). Upper Saddle River, NJ: Pearson Merrill Prentice Hall.

2. Beach, D., & Reinhartz, J. (1999). *Supervisory Leadership: Focus on Instruction* (1st ed.). Boston, MA: Allyn and Bacon.

3. Brookover, W. L., & Lezotte, L. W. (1977). *Changes in School Characteristics Coincident with Changes in Student Achievement.* Occasional Paper No. 17. East Lansing, MI: University Institute for Research on Teaching.

4. Maxwell, J., & Hoskins, R. (2021). *Change Your World: How anyone anywhere can make a difference.* Nashville, TN: Thomas Nelson.

5. Whitaker, T. (2013). *What Great Principals Do Differently: 18 Things That Matter Most* (2nd ed.). New York, NY: Routledge.

6. Wallace Foundation (2013). *The school principal: Guiding schools to better teaching and learning.* Retrieved from https://www.wallacefoundation.org/knowledge-center/Documents/The-School-Principal-as-Leader-Guiding-Schools-to-Better-Teaching-and-Learning-2nd-Ed.pdf.

7. Blase, J., & Blase, J. (2000, May). *Effective instructional leadership: Teachers' perspectives on how principals promote teaching and learning in schools.* Retrieved February 28, 2021 from https://researchgate.net/publication44826586_Effective_instructional_leadership_teachers'persprctives-on_how_principals_promote_teaching_and_learning-in_schools

Chapter Five

Teachers Need More Supervision, Not Evaluation

Today, more than ever, the practice of teacher evaluation has had such an urgent need to help teachers excel in the classroom to become dynamic teachers. As already stated in another chapter of this book, many teachers live and function in isolation. This chapter will focus on the fractured process of teacher supervision and evaluation. It is essential for those who consider themselves to be instructional leaders to focus on helping teachers improve every component of what teachers do in their classrooms as it relates to instruction.

This means if the desire is to see children in our schools excel to greater depths of learning, then principals must be intentional about this and function as instructional leaders, dedicating their time and energy to work with teachers to improve all aspects related to teaching. All educators should know that great teaching is affected by many variables, such as the overall school environment that is created from within the school, and at the same time, it must be understood that great teaching cannot be reduced to a prescription or a formula that applies to every teacher.

However, today this is being done in too many schools. It is an obligation and primary function of instructional leaders and teachers to be able to analyze teaching and have the skills necessary to work with each other in this process for the improvement of instruction. The field of supervision of instruction badly needs to be revisited. It is not about the evaluation models that many schools use today to assess teaching.

Millions of dollars are spent by states each year on these models, and these funds could easily be spent on other school initiatives that would be much more beneficial to schools than what these models provide. Schools are using these evaluation models as tools in their attempts to gauge and improve instruction, but it must be asked if these models are working, and if they are generating better instruction that fosters greater depths of student achievement.

Many would say these models are not generating the desired change that leads to the improvement of instruction that translates into great depths of student achievement. If these models are not providing the desired results, then something is either wrong with the models or they are not being used properly. In most cases, the manner in which they are used does not create better teaching and generates increased learning from students.

The New Teacher Project has a lot to say about excellence of instruction, and it should be reviewed and carefully studied by all teachers, instructional leaders, and those making policies relative to teaching and the assessment of it. This major report finds that effective teachers are the key to student success, yet school systems treat all teachers as interchangeable parts, not professionals. Excellence appears to be unrecognized and poor performance goes unaddressed.

This indifference to performance disrespects teachers and "gambles with students' lives."[1] If teachers are the key to student success, then it seems that schools should desire to do more to help teachers improve all aspects of what they do in the classroom. There are many things instructional leaders can use that support greater insights into what teachers do in the classroom and how they do it. Instructional leaders must know the *whats* and *hows* that make a difference in instruction.[2]

Quality supervision and evaluation must incorporate analysis of and reflection on teaching with significant information and feedback about how to improve the essence of teaching that supports greater depths of student engagement and learning.[3] This is needed today more than ever, but again, so many of those who are in positions to do this are stepping aside and not performing this extremely important and much needed function.

Without any doubt, the most important function of any school is to provide the best possible instruction it can for all students. This requires focus from those who are charged with making this happen, and they must be intentional about this and demonstrate complete and dedicated commitment to those things and processes that make instructional improvement become a reality in schools. This also necessitates continual professional support from those providing assistance and to those receiving it. In a school setting it is the teachers' and instructional leader's responsibility to make sure that significant gains are made in all aspects relating to instruction.

If a school is fortunate enough to have someone who is employed and dedicated to working with teachers as an instructional supervisor, that is good; however, in most schools, this is not the case. Therefore, the school principal must function as the instructional leader. It is this person who must provide support and help for all teachers and be deeply involved in the instructional process. Without this involvement, teachers will not receive the instructional support they desperately deserve and need.

SUPERVISION OR EVALUATION

This chapter will focus on the two most commonly used supervisory and evaluative techniques that are used in schools today and the benefits of each. For years research has continually provided evidence that great teaching is the most important factor that supports and affects student learning. If this is true, the preparation for instruction and the work teachers do in classrooms matters greatly, and the top priority for all schools should be to help and develop their teachers into becoming great teachers.

Focusing on teacher improvement should be the primary concern of every school, and improvement efforts should focus more on the formative aspects and not on the summative components related to teaching. Teacher improvement should occur in two phases that serve two distinctly different purposes but are directly tied to each other. The primary and most important phase should be concerned with observing teachers for developmental reasons that help them improve instructionally. This phase is called *formative assessment;* however, though many have used this type of assessment, it is not used enough today.

The second phase involves the use of data when making decisions about hiring or continuing a contract or granting merit awards. This is *summative assessment*.[4] In most cases, it is used more today than formative assessment, and it is believed to be more of a problem because it is not focused on helping teachers improve as much as formative assessment does. In most schools today, teacher evaluation procedures typically found can be classified as summative while evaluation that emphasizes ongoing growth and development would be considered formative.[5]

Summative assessment occurs more frequently because most states require summative, not formative. Again, it is time for policy makers and educators to begin to look at those things that have proven over and over again to attain greater results. This clearly means that legislatures, departments of education, and other policy makers begin to realize there is a better way to improve instructional practices than spending millions of dollars on an evaluation model that is either used inappropriately or does not generate the desired results.

In many places, this book discusses how mandates and policy makers comprise a huge part of the problem as it relates to the improvement of instruction. Their primary focus seems to be on the summative component of evaluation in which all teachers are given a score on their teaching, ranging from a score of one to five (1–5) that equates to teaching performance. It is a shame that in many cases, even school leaders who are trained in the process of using these models to assess teaching are told during the training that all teachers should start at least at a score of three out of five (1–5 score); teachers will eventually be assigned one of those scores with very little if any written comments from their school leader/principal.

When this occurs, it represents a totally wrong and an inappropriate method of working with teachers for instructional improvement purposes. The use of these evaluation checklists is often confusing and meaningless when the checklists are not designed to depict good practice. This approach to assessing teaching performance is limited in aiding teachers who need help and support. This lack of support further places them in a state of isolation and helplessness.

The current approach used by many schools ignores all the intricacies related to teacher effectiveness and overlooks the real purpose of helping teachers get better with the practices associated with great teaching. Regarding teacher effectiveness, even the developer of one of the most popular teacher evaluation models used in schools today to assess teacher performance indicates that most schools have interpreted the listing of instructional strategies and practices in this teacher evaluation model as absolutes. This developer and many others totally disagree with this concept.

It must be understood, there is no single instructional strategy or teacher evaluation model that can guarantee student learning.[6] It appears that many who are using this model (and similar models) to summatively assess and evaluate teaching have completely misinterpreted what the ultimate intensions were when this model and others were originally developed. Based on teacher effectiveness, it is easy to agree with the developer's comment.

If prescribed teaching and assessment are continued in the summative method of viewing and analyzing teaching, the same results will be produced, and administrators will continue looking for programs and models that do not fully work; students also will not receive appropriate learning opportunities. Some might say when using the teacher supervisory process that schools should go back to the basics, and that may be correct if it improves instructional practices that allow students to process what has been taught so they can apply it to new learning. It seems apparent today that many have forgotten what the basics really are.

This quantitative approach that leads to the scoring of teaching with a numerical number gives teachers very little information regarding teaching performance and even less regarding what they can do to improve their instructional skills. It also adds additional confusion as to what next steps can be taken to improve it. Since this score keeping of teaching does not seem to be working, it is time teaching is viewed as a supervisory function, and that means asking what can school leaders do to help teachers—not giving them a number related to their teaching performance that provides no help at all.

The instructional leader should interpret the supervisory process to mean, What can I as the instructional leader do to help you? This represents the first step in the formative process of helping teachers. It seems reasonable that observations of teachers for the purpose of assistance and helping them get better at teaching should be distinct from observations on which to base decisions about nonrenewal or renewal of a teaching contract.

Instructional leaders must understand that evaluation and supervision are two separate functions.[7] Supervisions' major focus should concern itself with improvement of classroom instruction, while administration as a function concerns itself with the overall operations of the school, including evaluating teacher performance.

It is easy to infer that if school leaders spent more time assisting teachers—rather than evaluating them—a higher quality of instruction could be attained. This would also create a situation where the school leader would work with teachers instead of engaging in the expensive (and often painful process) of releasing them and hiring another one. School leaders need to recognize that a teacher released from a contract will probably teach somewhere else. Is this exchange really helping the profession?

For the most part, teachers who are currently teaching will be teaching for years to come. Therefore, it seems logical that time would be spent on trying to help them improve, no matter where they are. Keeping teachers in effective service as growing professional educators should be one of the primary focuses of supervision.

Many believe the continuing failure to resolve the dilemma between teacher supervision and evaluation has created monumental challenges for those who practice instructional supervision.[8] This is truly unfortunate but completely true, and others agree with this comment, making the following statement:

> The evaluative function of supervision is historically rooted in bureaucratic, inspection-type supervision. Maintaining an effective and efficient school organization as well as a sound instructional program mandates that teachers are assessed for competence. In other words, the evaluative aspect of the supervisory function emanates from organizational requirements to measure and assess teaching effectiveness. The origins of the helping or improving function of supervision can be dated back to the early democratic practices in colonial America and later in the twentieth century. In other words, helping teachers to

improve instruction and promote pupil achievement grew out of the democratic theory of supervision. Supervisors or people concerned with supervision have faced a basic role conflict; namely, the unresolved dilemma between the necessity to evaluate (a bureaucratic function) and the desire to genuinely assist teachers in the instructional process (a professional goal).[9]

FORMATIVE VERSUS SUMMATIVE ASSESSMENT

Using this comment of "a professional goal" as a starting point, this assistance represents the ultimate intent of the instructional leader to work with teachers to help them improve their instruction. Therefore, it must be asked why this is not practiced more, especially since those who use this formative practice know it gets better results from teachers. If improving instruction is what is desired, then it is incumbent that instructional leaders spend more time on the formative components related to the supervisory process and not the summative practices that are so prevalent today in schools.

This would also require that policy makers need to understand and listen to those who do know how important formative assessment really is and how it can improve instructional practices. When formative assessment is used the way it is intended, it also can provide teachers excellent evidence regarding students in their classrooms and their learning needs. This is something that all schools need if their desire is to be truly successful.

Formative supervision is something that is done very little in our schools today. As already stated, it is understood the summative/evaluative process is usually required by policy; however, summative assessment as it is currently practiced in most schools today has proven that it does not promote the desired growth necessary for improving teaching. It is evaluation, not supervision.

It is essential that the supervisory process promote self-reflection so that teachers may learn more about why they do what they do and how they can adjust instructional practices as necessary for greater student engagement and achievement. It must be noted that many, if not all, of the summative types of assessments used today by schools also contain qualitative components that address what teachers actually do in the classroom and at what level they do them, but these qualitative components seem to get little consideration.

This is wrong and here is where many mistakes are made. To view an excellent example of how to use a formative assessment tool that exhibits great qualitative components that can be used to aid instructional improvement, textbox 5.1 can be extremely helpful in this endeavor. This textbox relates specifically to what teachers do in the classroom and at what level they are doing them. It does not include numerical values that mean nothing.

This formative assessment tool also includes a section that relates specifically to the classroom environment. Teachers can use this tool with each other, as they should be allowed to engage in collaborative peer observations with their teacher colleagues. This process of teachers observing teachers has proven to be extremely valuable and effective, and at the same time, allows them to demonstrate trust in each other and in the process of formative assessment.

TEXTBOX 5.1 TOOL FOR OBSERVATION OF PEERS SCORING RUBRIC

Jones: Teacher Observation Instrument
Tool for Observation of Peers (TOP)

This Tool for Observation of Peers (TOP) is an observational tool that can be used by instructional leaders or teacher colleagues for peer observation as they work together to improve instructional practices in schools. It is recommended that teachers use this TOP to formatively observe each other twice each year. Also attached is a rubric where observers can make comments relative to the TOP criteria. Observers and instructors should review the rubric carefully and consider the types of evidence needed to address each category. Peer observations are to be used to assist faculty in helping them to improve instructional skills and to demonstrate to students the teaching qualities and behaviors that are necessary for greater depths of student achievement.

The observer should:

- arrive before the class begins;
- bring a copy of the TOP and the TOP rubric;
- observe the class, paying attention to the ten TOP criteria teacher observations;
- provide evidence for each of the TOP criteria;
- provide suggestions or comments;
- discuss the observation and findings with the instructor after the class or at an agreed upon time;
- sign the TOP (optional); and
- provide a copy of the TOP for the instructor.

The instructor should:

- choose a class for the observer to attend;
- provide the observer with any materials needed for the class;
- discuss the observation and findings with the observer after the class or at an agreed upon time;
- sign the TOP (optional); and
- sign the TOP (optional—signature does not indicate agreement with the evaluation; signature indicates the TOP has been reviewed with the instructor).

Criteria

Instruction

	Levels of Performance			
1. Makes learning goals and instructional procedures clear to all students.	Students receive no information, confusing information, or inaccurate information about goals or students receive no information, confusing information, or inaccurate information about instructional procedures.	Students receive some information, and the information is accurate. However, the information is not sufficient for students to complete the activities.	Teacher provides clear, accurate information about instructional goals and procedures; most students seem to understand.	Students receive accurate information and seem to understand fully. All students, including those who have trouble initially, can carry out instructional procedures.	Teacher guides students through a constructive process of formulating goals and procedures. All students, including those who have trouble initially, can carry out instructional procedures.
2. Teaches concepts with depth and specificity; guides students through application and practice of concepts; content is based on most current research.	Content is inaccurate or appears incomprehensible to students.	Content is accurate. Content is not challenging, deep, or specific enough for the level of students.	Content is accurate. Instruction methods do not vary to address different learning styles.	Content is accurate and based on most current research. Instructional methods vary to address different learning styles.	Content is accurate and based on most current research. Instructional methods vary to address different learning styles. Content is deep, specific, and challenging. Lesson structure is logical and coherent.

3. Encourages students to perform at the high end of Bloom's Taxonomy; encourages higher order thinking skills.	Discourages independent and critical thinking. (Suggests there is only one "right" answer.)	Does not discourage higher order thinking. No evidence of encouraging higher order thinking.	Encourages critical, independent, and creative thinking within the context of the lesson.	Encourages critical, independent, and creative thinking within the context of the lesson. Uses teachable moments to extend thinking when possible.	Encourages critical, independent, and creative thinking through activities or strategies designed or chosen with this intent.
4. Monitors student understanding throughout the lesson; repeats and reteaches as necessary; adjusts lesson when necessary; provides substantive feedback frequently.	Student understanding is not monitored during the lesson. Feedback is not provided.	Student understanding is monitored somewhat during the lesson. Some points are repeated, but not taught from a fresh perspective. Feedback provided is not timely or substantive.	Student understanding is monitored during the lesson. Attempts are made to reteach, but not to the point that all students understand. Feedback is minimal.	Student understanding is monitored during the lesson. Teacher repeats and reteaches until most students understand. Feedback is timely, frequent, and substantive.	Student understanding is monitored during the lesson. Teacher repeats and reteaches until all students understand. Feedback is timely, frequent, and substantive. Teacher adjusts lesson when necessary.
5. Paces the lesson so that students remain engaged the entire class period; spends entire instructional time on activities of instructional value.	Substantial time is spent on activities of little instructional value or pacing is inappropriate for students or content.	Noninstructional activities are not efficient. Pacing is inappropriate for most students.	Instructional material is provided for the entire instructional period. Pacing is appropriate for most students.	Most students are engaged in activities of instructional value the entire period. Noninstructional activities are efficient. Pacing is appropriate for most students.	All students are engaged in activities of instructional value the entire period. Noninstructional activities are efficient. Pacing is appropriate.

Criteria

Environment

	Levels of Performance				
1. Models and encourages fairness, respect, acceptance, and open-mindedness among students.	Unfair to students or tolerates obviously unfair behavior among students	Fair to students. Does not model and encourage open-mindedness and acceptance.	Fair to students and does not tolerate unfair behavior among students. Does not model and encourage open-mindedness and acceptance.	Fair to students and does not tolerate unfair behavior among students. Models open-mindedness and acceptance.	Fair to students; actively encourages fairness and tolerance among students.
2. Creates and maintains rapport with students as a group and as individuals.	No attempts are made to establish rapport or inappropriate attempts are made.	Attempts are made to establish rapport with students as a group. Although attempts are appropriate, they do not appear successful.	A general level of rapport is reached with students as a group (eye contact, respect for student opinions, smiling, joking, etc.).	In addition to rapport with students as a group, the teacher establishes rapport with one individual student (draws on knowledge of that student's background and interests).	In addition to rapport with students as a group, the teacher establishes rapport with two or more individual students (draws on knowledge of those students' backgrounds and interests).
3. Communicates high learning expectations to all students.	Explicitly communicates low learning expectations.	Implicitly communicates low learning expectations.	Neutral, no negative effects.	Communicates high learning expectations to some students.	Actively communicates high learning expectations to *all* students.

4. Fosters appropriate, on-task behavior; consistently follows standards of behavior as stated in the syllabus.	Students are not consistently engaged with the material or disruptions are not addressed or standards for behavior from the syllabus are not followed.	Few students are not consistently engaged with the material or disruptions are addressed in an inappropriate manner.	Few disruptions to learning occur. When disruptions occur, they are addressed appropriately and with respect for the student.	Monitors student engagement with material. Addresses disruptions to learning appropriately and respectfully.	Student behavior is consistently appropriate and follows the standards in the syllabus or disruptions to learning are identified quickly through frequent monitoring and resolved appropriately and respectfully.
5. Uses the physical space as a resource to promote learning.	Allows unsafe conditions or environment interferes with learning.	Although no students appear to endanger themselves, there are potentially unsafe conditions. The environment may be distracting to some students.	Safe. Environment does not interfere with learning.	Safe. Some students' physical needs are accommodated. Teacher begins to adjust the environment to maximize resources.	Safe. If teacher cannot control conditions, he or she effectively adjusts activities for environment. Environment used as a resource and all students' needs accommodated.

Tool for Observation of Peers (TOP)

Instructor:	Date:	Observer:

Assessment Categories	Evidence or qualitative comments that support observations
INSTRUCTION	
1. Makes learning goals and instructional procedures clear to all students.	
2. Teaches concepts with depth and specificity; guides students through application and practice of concepts, and content is based on most current research.	
3. Encourages students to perform at the high end of Bloom's Taxonomy; encourages higher order thinking skills.	
4. Monitors student understanding throughout the lesson and repeats and reteaches as necessary; adjusts lesson when necessary; provides substantive feedback frequently.	
5. Paces the lesson so that students remain engaged the entire class period; spends entire instructional time on activities of instructional value.	
ENVIRONMENT	
1. Models and encourages fairness, respect, acceptance, and open-mindedness among students.	
2. Creates rapport with students as a group and as individuals.	
3. Communicates high learning expectations to all students.	
4. Fosters appropriate, on-task behavior; consistently follows standards of behavior as stated in the syllabus.	
5. Uses the physical space as a resource to promote learning.	

Overall suggestions and comments: _____
_____
_____
_____

Many speak about using formative assessment; however, talk is cheap, as very few do use it. Formative assessment is a nonnegotiable for school instructional leaders, and there are four guidelines that encompass when it is used:

- formative assessment should be a daily part of instruction,
- formative assessment should be intentional,
- formative assessment can be informal, and
- formative assessment should be used to guide instruction.[10]

Agreeing with these nonnegotiables should not be a problem for school leaders, but it seems it is since most who are charged with leading and guiding instructional practices today are not using it to assist teachers. When used properly, it has proven over and over to be an extremely important and positive step in helping teachers improve their instructional skills.

Therefore, if improving instruction is what is desired, then it seems apparent that instructional leaders should allow teachers to work collaboratively together to help each other by spending greater time themselves on the formative aspects of supervision. In almost every situation when formative assessment has been implemented properly, it gets great results; teachers should help each other in this process. Again, formative assessment of instruction is something that occurs infrequently in schools today.

One dynamic way of accomplishing this collaborative process is to allow seasoned veteran teachers to observe first- or second-year teachers and give them sufficient time for several observations. At the same time, the seasoned teachers should be observed by those they are observing. Once this process takes place, it is also important to give the teachers who are working together in this process sufficient time to visit together about their observation(s).

It should also be considered to give those who are doing the observations the time to share their experiences in faculty meetings. Allowing this helps to create buy in from others, and this adds value to the formative process and can encourage others to get involved as well. For this process to work properly and effectively, sufficient time must be dedicated for the formative assessment of teaching.

Instructional leaders must place greater emphasis on formative assessment and remember that formative teacher assessment is a supervisory function intended to assist teachers in professional growth and for the improvement of teaching.[11] Through formative assessment, the focus is on the needs of the teacher—specifically, on teaching and learning.

There are major differences between formative and summative assessment and instructional leaders must learn to adapt the use of these two approaches and more specifically, they should use more formative assessment as they work with first-year teachers. All learning opportunities need to be formative and continuous. There are five formative approaches that can be used in schools today to assist teachers in classroom performance. It is safe to say these approaches should and could be used with seasoned teachers as well. This list includes the following formative approaches to working with teachers:

- Frequent contact—All teachers need frequent contact from supervisors and teacher colleagues for support and to review instructional practices
- Balanced supervision—This begins when school starts, and it is both formal and informal visits that continue throughout the school year
- Goal setting—Goals for teaching should be set at the beginning of the year that allow for coordinating efforts that will impact teaching
- Focus classroom observation—This allows for focused classroom observations based on an identified area from a pre-conference that demonstrates a need for assistance
- Differentiated approaches—This approach can consist of action research, portfolio development, and peer coaching[12]

There potentially are other formative approaches to use with teachers, but this gives school leaders and teachers an excellent example of formative approaches that will work and support collegiality and instructional improvement.

TYPE OF FORMATIVE SUPERVISION THAT GETS RESULTS

As stated previously, it is reasonable to believe that observations of teachers for the purpose of assistance should be distinct from observations on which to base decisions about nonrenewal or renewal of a teaching contract. Improving the effectiveness of teaching is the central purpose of the supervisory process. This also means supervision is to become a dynamic process and oriented to improve teaching in ways that can be perceived.[13]

This statement has strong merit, but instead of being merely perceived, improvement of teaching must show visible signs of progress that are observable. Educators must break away from traditional approaches to supervision and find ways that will lead supervision toward improving instruction.

There are many approaches that can be used formatively, but one approach that has been found to be very helpful and effective is *clinical supervision*. It is an approach that has proven to be extremely effective for improving instruction. Scholars who have studied and researched clinical supervision's effectiveness have found that in every situation when it has been used properly, it has provided positive results.

Primarily, clinical supervision is an observation process where a teacher is being observed by a colleague or instructional leader who serves as a mirror and confidant, and who works with the teacher to critically look at and review instructional practices, providing support that allows for changes to be made that are needed for improvement purposes.

It must be clearly understood that clinical supervision is not a program that schools buy; therefore, it is not something that is forced on teachers. Since it is not a program or model that is purchased, using it will save school districts millions of dollars. Those dollars could easily be spent on something else that could better benefit schools.

However, it does take time to utilize clinical supervision. Therefore, some of the funds spent on evaluation models could be spent on hiring instructional supervisors who could work with teachers using the clinical supervision process. Four of the basic components that encompass clinical supervision are:

- Pre-observation conference—During the pre-conference, the teacher/supervisor/colleague collaboratively determines the purpose and focus of the observation. This could involve discussing student learning outcomes, or it could focus on instructional practices used. Also, discussion should occur about how and what types of data will be collected.
- Observation of the lesson—When conducting the lesson observation, the observer should develop a general description of the observed lesson, and the collection of observation data should apply to strengths and weaknesses observed.
- Analysis and interpretation of data—This allows the observer to dedicate time to analyze the observation data and indicate findings interpreted from this analysis in terms of best practices for student learning, instructional strengths, and areas in need of improvement. Once completed, it is used for the post-conference.
- Post-conference and critique—This conference is used for discussion of observation data, analysis, and interpretation and teacher feedback. It should also provide information regarding how to collaboratively design a professional growth plan designed from research on student learning for the teacher.

Clinical supervision is designed to enable educators to improve instructional behavior more effectively. It is collegial and does not have a "got you" mentality. Clinical supervision seeks to foster some change in teaching to show that a change did in fact take place by comparing the former and the new patterns of instruction. These patterns should give teachers greater insight into their teaching.

Completely in line with clinical supervision, instructional leaders and teachers should be aware there are several guiding principles that should be kept in mind when observing teachers and working with them to assist them in their instructional endeavors. Four of these principles are clarified here:

- Good supervision is about engaging teachers in reflective thinking and discussion based on insightful and useful observation, not on evaluation.
- Observation is a two-step process: first, to describe what has occurred, and second, to interpret what it means.
- Supervision that relies on observation instruments that generates usable data about what is taking place in the classroom can be used by teachers to improve their instructional skills by allowing them to practice what the collected data verified that needed improvement.
- Observing takes skills and practice. Quite often individuals interpret as they observe. If tools of observation are to be effective, then observers must practice separating interpretation from description.[14]

In summary, clinical supervision, if done properly, does have a positive impact on instructional practices, and it can be perceived by students, teachers, and by those colleagues observing them. Another great thing that clinical supervision improves is the instructional leader's or colleague's observing supervisory skills. It is highly recommended that clinical supervision be used much more in schools because it does foster better teaching that supports greater depths of student achievement.

CONCLUDING THOUGHTS

It is hoped that educators, especially those who are charged to assess instructional performance of teachers, will understand that traditional supervision as most practice today is not supervision at all. In most cases, as already stated, its attention focuses on mandated procedures and policies, which school leaders must discharge as they formally evaluate teachers. Usually, it is performed to determine whether or not a teacher meets certain performance standards the state has adopted and says they must meet.

Terms and phrases often heard in this traditional and formalistic approach are: teacher competencies, performance objectives, and assessment. If the current models used by school districts today are supposed to improve instruction, then why does the profession still have teachers who have not improved sufficiently and are in need of help? It is easy to place the blame on the models schools choose to use to assess teaching performance, but those who embrace the title of instructional leader should be held accountable as well.

It must be asked by instructional leaders and policy makers if the models being used today to assess and evaluate instruction are not producing the desired effect. If so, then what is being used is broken and cannot remedy the problem. To reinforce previous comments made earlier in this chapter, the summative evaluative process is usually required by policy, but in most cases, this process does not promote the desired growth that is necessary for improving teaching.

It is evaluation, not supervision. It is essential that the supervisory process promote self-reflection and for teachers to learn more about why they do what they do and can make adjustments as necessary for greater student engagement and achievement. With that said, what is it teachers need from those who assess their instruction? For years, as shown in studies of the practice of supervision and evaluation, most K–12 schools have shortchanged the supervision/helping component and focused almost exclusively instead on state-mandated evaluation/summative procedures that rarely seem to support and promote instructional improvement.

This purely summative focus must change if the desired effect of improved instruction is truly expected from teachers and desired from students. Scholarly research strongly supports this change and further shows the desired results are not being achieved. As already stated, one of the many challenges faced by school leaders today is they are required to follow the law or policy regarding teacher evaluation/assessment, which completely detracts from what should be done to help teachers improve teaching that supports students' academic needs and success.

This focus has created significant challenges in helping teachers, but the truly great instructional leaders do spend considerable time working with teachers to improve the essence of instruction, no matter what the challenges may be. As indicated in the research on this topic, the intent of instructional supervision is to promote teacher growth and expertise. This means that teacher supervision should be an organizational function concerned with teacher growth, leading to improvement in teaching performance and greater student learning.[15]

Most school leaders use the same approach and supervisory methods that they would use to supervise and assess all teachers. It does not matter if they are first-year teachers, mid-career, or well-seasoned teachers. This singular approach is not an effective method to use while working with teachers to improve the overall quality of instruction. One size does not fit all. This concept goes completely against what great instructional leaders should do as they work with their teachers.

Most school leaders claim to place great value on teaching, but if teaching is truly valued, then assessment must be valued as well—and conducted properly. Working with teachers to improve instruction should be a supportive and helpful process, and at times, the process must be differentiated depending on individual teacher needs. School leaders are educators and are smart enough to know what great teaching looks like; they should be able and willing to work with teachers personally or allow teachers to work collaboratively with each other to help improve instruction.

The question must be asked, Does it always take a program or model forced upon teachers? It is time schools start doing things to assist and to help teachers, instead of throwing models and programs at them that are here today and gone tomorrow. This proves these programs and models are truly ineffective. If the current models used by school districts are supposed to improve instruction, then why are teachers allowed to continue teaching if their teacher evaluations are consistently not effective? Again, is this what is truly desired out of the evaluation models that schools are required to use as the source to assess instruction?

If it is, then the system is seriously broken and those in positions of authority who make these decisions for schools have no idea about what is best for improving instructional practice and how to do it. Supporting this statement is the NEA's White Paper Report, which states the current systems in place for assessing, evaluating, and supporting teachers too often fail to improve teacher practices and enhance student growth and learning.[16]

Based on reports and comments from teachers and principals, this is an unfortunate finding. Therefore, one of two situations are occurring: principals are afraid to address the situation with a marginally underperforming teacher, or the model is not being used properly. Regarding this, the following questions must be asked by educators and policy makers:

- What should schools do to improve instruction?
- How does a school know if teaching is having a positive impact on student achievement?
- What is it that teachers need from supervision and evaluation?
- What do teachers need from instructional leaders relating to instructional help and support?

These four questions are extremely valid for schools today, but the leadership function has changed greatly, and one of the major contributors and causes of these changes are the models and programs that have been developed and inserted into many of the things leaders do with teachers. In many cases, it appears that everything relating to instructional improvement has significantly changed for the worst and digressed from what used to be completed with and for teachers— it now has changed to what is done to teachers.

For the educational leadership function, this brings into play what many would refer to as summative assessment, as discussed in this chapter. State departments of education and national and state leaders have come to believe it is about using a program or model to assess and even improve instruction. In many situations, this belief and practice of these programs and models have caused the elimination of all the components relating to formatively working with teachers to analyze and improve instructional practices.

It is extremely important to note and understand that three to four decades ago, most school leaders spent considerable time in classrooms observing teaching, classroom management skills, and student involvement in instructional dialogue. School leaders were instructional leaders and spent this time in classrooms because they knew that was where everything occurred, and they could see instruction improving as well as student learning. In addition, during this time frame, most school districts developed their own evaluation/assessment instruments.

School leaders knew their primary purpose was to work with teachers to improve the essence of teaching. They also knew if they were in classrooms, discipline problems were minimized. They could see if courses were taught in ways to meet all learners' needs, but most importantly, they could visually observe what teachers needed to focus on relative to what was being taught and what was happening in the classroom. This represented an excellent example of formative assessment.

This formative practice was effective, and if practiced today, it would still be effective. However, for the most part, this extremely important function has disappeared, and teachers seem to be starving for help, which includes the need for assistance with classroom management skills. In many ways, this could be the reason the educational system has developed into a profession where fewer individuals aspire to be teachers and school leaders. Over time many things have changed, but one of the most important changes has been how school leaders commit less time to working with teachers to improve instructional practices.

Instructional leaders must understand, before they can assess teaching, they must learn it requires them to be in classrooms more than they currently are. They must be able to collect data about what happens in the classroom and discuss this data with teachers for the express purpose of improving teaching performance. This includes observing and listening carefully to the interactions teachers are having with students.

As said previously, maybe it is time schools return "back to the basics." By doing this, schools could possibly start seeing what everyone desires to see, and that desire must focus on instructional leadership that promotes better instruction to support greater depths of student engagement and learning. This needed change in direction will support collegiality with and between teachers and students and will enhance and improve instruction in the school.

NOTES

1. Weisberg, D., Sexton, S., Mulhern, J., & Keeling, D. (2009). *The Widget Effect*. Retrieved September 7, 2018 from https://tntp.org/assets/documents/TheWidgetEffect_execsummary_2nd_ed.pdf.

2. Glickman, C. C., Gordon, Stephen P., & Ross-Gordon, J. M. (2014). *Supervision and instructional leadership: A developmental approach* (9th ed.). Boston, MA: Pearson.

3. Weisberg, D., Sexton, S., Mulhern, J., & Keeling, D. (2009). *The Widget Effect*. Retrieved from https://files.eric.ed.gov/fulltext/ED515656.pdf.

4. Beach, D., & Reinhartz, J. (1999). *Supervision: Focus on instruction*. Boston, MA: Allyn and Bacon.

5. Sergiovanni, T. J., & Starratt, R. J. (2006). *Supervision: A redefinition* (8th ed.). New York, NY: McGraw-Hill.

6. Marzano, R. J. (2017). *The new art and science of teaching*. Bloomington, IL: Solution Tree.

7. Glickman, C. D., Gordon, S. P., & Ross-Gordon, J. M. (1997). *Supervision of Instruction: A developmental approach* (9th ed.). Upper Saddle River, NJ: Prentice Hall.

8. Nolan, J. F., & Hoover, L. A. (2011). *Teacher supervision and evaluation: Theory into practice* (3rd ed.). Hoboken, NJ: John Wiley & Sons.

9. Glanz, J. (1998). Histories, antecedents, and legacies of school supervision. In G. Firth and E. Pajak (Eds.), *Handbook of research on school supervision* (pp. 39–79). New York: Macmillan Library Reference.

10. Martin, J. (2020). *Turning a school around: Key considerations for real success*. New York, NY: Rowman & Littlefield.

11. Glickman, C. D., Gordon, S. P., & Ross-Gordon, J. M. *Supervision of instruction: A developmental approach.* (10th ed.) Boston, MA: Pearson.

12. Zepeda, S. J. (2013). *The principal as instructional leader: A practical handbook* (3rd ed.). New York, NY: Routledge.

13. Harris, B. M. (1985). *Supervisory behavior in education* (3rd ed.). Englewood Cliffs, NJ: Prentice-Hall.

14. Sullivan, S., & Glanz, J. (2013). *Supervision that improves teaching: Strategies and techniques* (4th ed.). Thousand Oaks, CA: Corwin Press.

15. Nolan, J. F., & Hoover, L. A. (2011). *Teacher supervision and evaluation theory into practice* (3rd ed.). Hoboken, NJ: John Wiley and Sons.

16. *NEA's white paper report*. (2010). Retrieved October 10, 2020 from https://eric.ed.gov/?id=EJ773253.

Chapter Six

Redefining Professional Development

There is no doubt, schools must provide better professional development for teachers; it is the instructional leader's responsibility to know what each teacher's needs are and how to provide those needs that are specific to what teachers do in the classroom. It is critical for an instructional leader to find time during work in the school environment to help teachers develop professionally.

The vast majority of highly qualified educators believe it is important for teachers to understand time will be set aside and dedicated to their professional learning.[1] School-embedded professional development should be an expectation as well as an opportunity for teachers and instructional leaders to collaboratively discuss teaching and learning that sets the stage for the refinement and improvement of teaching and pedagogical skills.

It is sad to say that this is not done very much today; it is a huge area that goes unaddressed and continuously causes major problems in helping teachers improve their instructional skills that would improve everything they do as they teach their students. This means schools must provide better professional development for teachers, and it must be of a quality to be usable by them as they work daily to improve their instructional expertise.

All schools should desire to have teachers who are inspired to teaching excellence. When this happens, students will also be inspired to excellence as well. Most individuals in other professions have continuing professional development opportunities that support what their profession requires of them. The harsh truth is that staff development is a low priority in most schools today.[2]

Schools are vital places for teaching and learning. A school's vitality is assessed by the vitality of its teachers and, ultimately, by those charged with leading schools. This vitality can then be transferred to every student, giving them the skills they need to succeed and to feel great about their success. However, schools must see and recognize this and make sure this transfer takes place in every classroom.

According to one of the largest research studies ever conducted regarding professional development, schools are not using professional development as effectively as they should. It also provided evidence that many school districts are spending vast amounts of money on professional development for their teachers each year, with some districts averaging $18,000 per teacher. The report further says that improvements in teacher development are not occurring, which in turn, shows a lack of improvement in student success.[3]

In addition, this suggests schools need to stop how they are currently approaching professional development and instead redefine, reevaluate, and reinvent it so schools can see yearly professional growth from their teachers. Once this takes place, it will translate into better teaching that supports student learning. School leaders should be involved in discussions with their teachers, asking questions about what would make professional development more effective and get the results they want it to have.

First and foremost, a needs assessment must be taken regarding what teachers desire from school-embedded professional development that is provided by the school. So much money appears to be wasted by school districts providing professional development for their teachers, and it seems the majority of teachers have no interest in or already have enough knowledge of the content that is presented in these professional development sessions.

According to what are considered powerful learning practices, teachers need a voice and choice rather than a one-size-fits-all approach to professional development, as the great teachers know they must differentiate instruction in efforts to reach all students.[4] Teachers desire school-embedded professional development that helps them become better teachers—not just for fulfilling the state requirement regarding the allotment of time that is required by so many states and schools today.

This means teachers are interested in growing over time, and this growth will allow them to make connections with each other and then transfer those learned connections into their own classrooms. Without any doubt, effective school-embedded professional development is content focused, incorporates active learning, supports collaboration, uses models of effective practice, provides coaching and expert support, offers feedback and reflection, and is of sustained duration.

This means teachers crave professional development that is hands-on, collaborative, and regularly supported until they know they are implementing new and learned skills effectively into the classroom. To ensure a coherent system that supports teachers across the entire professional continuum, professional learning should link to their experiences in preparation and induction, as well as to teaching standards and evaluation.[5]

It should also bridge to leadership opportunities to ensure a comprehensive system that is focused on the growth and development of teachers. At the same time, the professional learning provided to teachers can be more effective if teachers are allowed to give feedback regarding the professional development provided by schools. However, in most cases this is never done.

As stated earlier in this chapter, schools should seek guidance and direction from their teachers regarding what type of school-embedded professional development is needed to support what teachers do. Once this takes place, the professional development should then be assessed by teachers to see if it is preparing them sufficiently and providing the desired results. However, in most situations, there appears to be a lack of systematic evaluation efforts after the professional development is offered.

What good does it do if there is no plan in place to not only evaluate the training but also to evaluate the implementation and progress made after the training? To determine what teachers are saying about the effectiveness of the professional development provided to them, one can use the survey in textbox 6.1, which can be tremendously beneficial when teachers are afforded the opportunity to complete it.

Using feedback will give instructional leaders much needed information from their teachers about how the professional development helped them perform better—if it actually did help them. It will also be a great source of information regarding what their teachers do need if it did not help them. This provision is a must, and if the leader is leading and in classrooms on a regular basis, this will give them a better understanding of what help their teachers need to become as successful as possible.

If school leaders are fully engaged in this very important process, they will definitely see instructional improvement. This also affords school leaders direct access to what each teacher needs relating to school-embedded professional development. This will also give leaders an understanding regarding why modifications to professional development are necessary and are relevant to teachers and the teaching process.

For years, professional development has fixated on what has been defined as bringing expertise to teachers through group presentations or some type of group workshop. Quality professional development should emphasize building a culture that has a clear and shared purpose that supports and improves teacher development.[6] If this is done properly, it allows schools to focus on teacher needs and student learning outcomes. This also allow schools to place emphasis on specific skills that teachers need and strategies that support those needs.

TEXTBOX 6.1. JONES PROFESSIONAL DEVELOPMENT QUESTIONNAIRE (JPDQ)

Please read each of the following descriptions of professional development activities provided by your school or district and how they support teaching that enhances student learning. In the right margin, circle the number that you feel most nearly describes the extent to which you believe the professional development activities/training assist you as a teacher.

The following are definitions for the responses:

4 = ALWAYS (met my needs in every situation)
3 = USUALLY (commonly or ordinarily presented material was helpful and usable)
2 = SELDOM (in few instances, rarely, infrequently)
1 = NEVER (at no time, under no conditions)

Circle the number that you believe represents your belief about the professional development (PD) provided by your school/district.

A. Participant Satisfaction	Circle One			
1. The PD activities are well organized.	4	3	2	1
2. The PD training make sense.	4	3	2	1
3. The trainer(s) is knowledgeable about materials presented.	4	3	2	1
4. The PD is useful for teachers and teaching.	4	3	2	1
5. The objectives of the PD are clearly defined.	4	3	2	1
6. The PD is relevant and supportive to what I do as a teacher.	4	3	2	1
B. Impact on Professional Practice				
7. The materials presented have a positive impact on my teaching.	4	3	2	1
8. The PD that is provided has a positive impact on student learning.	4	3	2	1
9. Teachers can effectively apply content learned from PD to instruction.	4	3	2	1
10. The PD presented enhances my professional growth.	4	3	2	1
11. The PD provided is something all teachers should have.	4	3	2	1
12. The PD enhances my professional growth and deepens my reflection and self-assessment of exemplary practices.	4	3	2	1
13. The PD allows me to gain several ideas I can embed in my teaching.	4	3	2	1
14. The PD provides skills I need to help me analyze and use data in decision making for improving my instruction.	4	3	2	1

Comments: _____
_____

If school leaders ever desire professional development to be applicable to what teachers do and what expertise they want teachers to possess, they must thoughtfully address the professional development they are providing and the expertise they want teachers to acquire from it. There are several dimensions of expertise that teachers should attain through professional training, but the three below seem to be absolutes:

- Professional expertise is the accumulation and use of certain technical skills.
- Professional expertise is the development and application of conceptual, general principles, and theories.
- Professional expertise is the ability in deliberate action.[7]

It must be understood, as things change in education, so the expertise of educators must change. Teachers are employed with a wealth of knowledge and skills, and those skills must continually be redefined and updated because the improvements needed in schools must continually meet the needs of students. Therefore, instructional leaders in schools must understand that the expertise and professional development teachers need must be continually improving, and they must look for changes that are absolutely needed by teachers. This requires instructional leaders to be intentional in their endeavors by creating a culture that supports continuous growth and learning for teachers.

CREATING A CULTURE THAT SUPPORTS CONTINUOUS LEARNING FOR TEACHERS

The concept of the principal functioning as the instructional leader of the school is nothing new; however, many principals fail to function in this capacity. Functioning in this capacity also requires them to be a developer of their teachers by recognizing and creating a culture in the school that supports continuous improvements that directly manifest in teaching and learning. The best teachers in schools today understand their content and how their students learn. To an instructional leader, observing teachers grow and mature in their instructional skills is just as exciting as observing students grow in their comprehension of content knowledge and its application to new learning.

The best way for teachers to continue growing and learning is for the school to provide the professional development that supports that growth. Teachers deserve the best professional development that schools can provide, and it needs to be flexible enough to meet each teacher's needs. In the eyes of many teachers today, schools completely fail to provide the professional development that truly supports the work they do.

In numerous conversations with teachers about the professional development provided to them by their schools, there has been a tendency to complain and place labels on the professional development provided to them; these labels appear to be very sad. The list of complaints regarding what teachers say of professional development are as follows:

- "drive-by" workshops
- one-size-fits-all presentations
- "been there, done that" topics
- little or no modeling of what is being taught
- lack of follow-up[8]

This is indeed horrible, and this must stop if schools ever hope to provide the help teachers truly need. For decades, school-embedded professional development has consisted of bringing some "expert" to the school to deliver a presentation about some area the district felt was important to teachers for their development. However, most teachers have not benefited from this.

This form of professional development provided to teachers should change from this format to emphasize the development of cultures within the school that have clear and shared purposes that support and nurture teacher development.[9] This relates specifically to what teachers do in the classroom, especially as they focus on student learning outcomes. Doing this allows teachers to work with and support each other by allowing inquiry into the teaching and learning process.

These complaints leave teachers with the feeling of isolation, of being treated unprofessionally, and of not being valued for what they are trying to do. The value of professional development in schools today simply cannot be measured by teachers attending a professional development training session that was provided by the school district. The question that must be asked is if these training sessions were effective and facilitated better instruction from teachers that increased higher levels of performance from students. If it did not and it could not be determined that the teaching improved, leading to greater depths of student achievement, it was a failure.

Most school districts are required to offer certain types of professional development to their teachers, and most of the time it does not cover the relevant content teachers need to help them improve their instructional skills; therefore, this type of professional development is insufficient and does not meet teachers' needs. It is the quality of the professional development that counts, not the quantity. Professional development must be focused on two distinct features: (1) the improvement of instruction that leads to (2) greater depths of student achievement. Every school/district leader and teacher should ask themselves if the schools in their district are meeting these two distinct features.

If these two features are not being attained in schools with the professional development that is being provided to teachers, the district and its schools are failing to address the overall needs of its schools. Quality professional development must happen in real time in schools, and it should be structured more for teams of teachers who can collaboratively work together and challenge each other to achieve excellence in teaching.

Once this process is realized and takes place in schools, it then must be structured and focused to improve student learning. It is the primary responsibility of the instructional leader to make sure this is happening in schools. This means principals cannot shirk their responsibility if they are truly an instructional leader. Instructional leaders are the major force in schools today who must recognize and be able to see their teachers receive the required support and learning opportunities they need to enhance student learning.

This does require them to be in classrooms much more than most currently are. Being in classrooms will also give them the opportunity to see how teachers are implementing the professional development that was provided to them. When this begins to take place in schools, they become dynamic, and change can take place that allows schools to make a positive difference in teachers', staff's, and students' lives.

Dynamic schools are schools that take charge of change.[10] This means change is not dictated from others who have never done what teachers and leaders do daily. School-embedded professional development is a clear example of dynamic change occurring in schools. This type of change allows schools to grow, with the goal of improving everything that is done in them. However, very few school leaders fail to understand this desired change also requires them to be invested in what teachers are doing in the classroom.

As already stated, they must be in classrooms on a regular basis, not just to perform the required summative evaluation of teachers but to assist, support, and—if necessary—to help redirect instruction. Great instructional leaders understand that frequent classroom visits allow them to truly know what teachers' needs are and assist them in providing the type of school-embedded professional development teachers must have.

If the instructional leader is providing the proper support and developing the proper culture in their school that supports teacher development, they will make sure it involves the following three professional development components:

- Sufficient time must be dedicated for teachers to reflect on their teaching.
- School-embedded professional development should be structured around teaching/learning needs specific to the school.
- Teachers should be given opportunities to plan and work together.

It is important to focus on teacher and student needs as school-embedded professional development is assessed in every school. When understanding and utilizing these three professional development needs in the proper manner, the school has the potential to come together in a fashion that will allow teachers and students to receive the benefit, and teaching and learning will be enhanced.

Sufficient Time Must Be Dedicated for Teachers to Reflect on Teaching

Great instructional leaders understand and recognize that teachers need time to reflect on their own teaching. It cannot be a once and done event. It also serves as a primary process for teachers spending sufficient time on addressing any concerns or modifications they could link to their teaching. This signifies to the teacher that the instructional leader understands teachers are the only person responsible for improving their own instructional skills. This allows teachers to correct any deficiencies they may have without potential reemployment issues.

Restructuring Professional Development to Meet Teacher's Needs

Instructional leaders must have high expectations for everyone in the school. High expectations and priorities mean instructional leaders and their faculty place value in what they are doing. This suggests that continuous efforts are needed to improve teaching and learning goals. With these expectations come assessment, and that means if the school places value in the expectations it has for teaching and learning, the school will then assess the teaching and learning components in multiple ways to see if they are obtaining the necessary outcomes. The success of the expectations for teaching and learning should not be based solely on teaching practices that may change, but more so on determining if the essence and application of learning has increased.

Giving Teachers Opportunities to Plan and Work Together

This book has stated many times that many teachers live in isolation and living there is wrong. Therefore, it is imperative for schools to dedicate time for teachers to spend together for sharing ideas, cultivating and developing differentiated teaching strategies that focus on improvement of teaching and enhancement of student learning. Time spent together as teachers developing these strategies allows them to ask thoughtful questions that can provide positive dialogue about tying teaching and learning goals together. It also gives them opportunities to discuss what the school is all about and what can make it better.

This team approach is crucial and enables teachers to grow together as a faculty, also giving them opportunities to make improvements together. Instructional leaders should create blocks of time dedicated for teachers to discuss lessons and to share expertise with each other. One great way for school leaders to use this team approach to give teachers opportunities to work together is by creating teams of teachers in their schools.

This can easily be done at the beginning of the school year if school leaders will give teachers an opportunity to share with each other at a faculty meeting what they consider to be their individual area of proficiency. One great way to accomplish this is for school leaders to develop a survey that can be distributed to teachers early in the year; this will allow teachers the opportunity to share with their teacher colleagues what their proficiency area is.

Once school leaders have this information, they can share it with their teachers. Then teachers can begin to visit with each other about those strengths that might help them individually. Textbox 6.2 can be very beneficial in assisting in this endeavor.

After carefully analyzing the results of the survey, school leaders and teachers can then use the results to allow them to work with other teachers who can help them in areas where they may need support and help. This is an excellent way to provide for school-embedded professional development that

---

TEXTBOX 6.2: JONES FACULTY PROFICIENCY SURVEY

Faculty, as you know, we update our faculty proficiency data at the beginning of each year. Please look carefully at the items below and put an X in the space that you believe is an area you are proficient in and would be willing to allow other faculty to visit with you about this area. Please add any area(s) that are not listed.

1. ___ Designing and implementing student collaborative teams
2. ___ Classroom management issues and concerns
3. ___ Adapting course content for all learners
4. ___ Working with parents/guardians
5. ___ Creating strong relationships with students
6. ___ Differentiated instruction for individual student needs
7. ___ Teaching that supports mastery learning
8. ___ Applying content standards to courses
9. ___ Managing and monitoring student learning
10. ___ Using technology that supports learning
11. ___ Other and explain _____

teachers have participated in from the beginning, and now they can begin to put it into practice. Again, this should be part of the school-embedded professional development program.

To support this form of school-embedded professional development, instructional leaders should consider creating common planning times for teachers to visit and to share with each other what they have observed and what their future plans are for their classes, relating to teaching and learning. These common planning times are crucial to the overall improvement of instruction in schools.

These common planning times also enable the instructional leader to bring different curricular programs together so teachers can talk about cross curricular components that allow them the opportunity to visit with those teachers who are not in their specific content teaching area. This gives teachers a chance to view and discuss different teaching styles and techniques that may not be used in the content area in which they currently teach.

Most of the time, the professional development that is provided are ubiquitous, wide-spread and one-shot, in-service workshops that have proven to achieve neither effective changes in teaching practices nor improvements in student learning.[11] These workshops that schools refer to as "professional development training sessions" for teachers usually focus on transmitting information that, for the most part, is not structured for teacher improvement and student learning. It is time for schools and districts to structure professional development on a continuous basis that allows for serious critiquing of the practices used for teaching.

At the same time, teachers must be allowed to share ideas with each other and allowed to spend time collaboratively discussing teaching techniques and learning. Once this is done, teachers will begin to create new strategies that support their learning, which can then be translated into the classroom. If educators truly desire to improve schools, they must begin to measure the professional development provided by schools to see how it improves instructional practices. If they do not do this, then it is apparent that all they want to do is to meet policy and mandate requirements. This is tragic and another example of schools coasting to an outcome that has no meaningful ending.

Professional development that is provided by schools must be an integral part of a systems perspective and systemic change efforts, with the most critical being the match between learning and teacher development. In addition, teacher development plans should contain the following components:

- individual development and organizational development;
- a clear plan that supports professional development;
- a focus on student needs and learning outcomes;

- multiple forms of job-embedded learning;
- study by teachers of the teaching and learning process;
- staff developers providing consultation, planning, and facilitation, as well as training;
- critical function and major responsibility of all administrators and teacher leaders;
- continuous improvement for everyone who effects students' learning; and
- an indispensable process for reform.[12]

Focus group meetings with teachers throughout the country have found that teachers need professional development that has these characteristics:

- Relevant—it is personalized with usable content for classrooms
- Interactive—contains strategies that teachers could use immediately
- Delivery—is delivered by someone who understands what teachers do
- Sustainable—something that is usable over a long period of time
- Professional treatment—treat teachers as professionals[13]

After reviewing what these components tell educators, it is apparent that professional development should not be viewed as something that is not important; however, most schools treat it that way. Schools must stop providing professional development that relates to the latest and supposedly greatest thing that is to improve the landscape of teaching and learning. This must change, and it must be understood that providing quality professional development that has a positive impact on teaching and learning is crucial in schools.

It is time for educational instructional leaders to recognize that teachers need the necessary skills and abilities associated with what they do in their classrooms. Policy makers have failed to understand this, and if schools continue failing to meet the learning needs of teachers, then teachers will not be able to sufficiently meet the learning needs of their students and will never accept the professional development that is provided for them.

TEACHER ACCEPTANCE

Acceptance from teachers is an essential component of getting any professional development program or activity to succeed in any school. If school leaders cannot get teachers to support and gladly participate in the professional development provided to them, that program is doomed to failure from the start. Teachers must see what is presented to them as necessary as well as something that will allow them to sharpen their teaching skills to help them promote student learning.

In many states, professional development is something that is required by state statute, and teachers tend to view it as a task to be completed to get enough points to check off a box as "completed." Teachers perceive this as a meaningless task that presents itself as a nuisance and is nonproductive for what they do as teachers. One of the best ways to target the professional development that teachers need is to simply ask them what training they need to support what they do in the classroom. No one knows more about what students need to be successful in the classroom than teachers.

If school leaders are just doing routine staff development to meet state mandates and requiring the latest trendy method of doing something, it is meaningless and will have no long-lasting positive impact on teaching and learning. As previously mentioned, surveying teachers and asking them what they need is a valuable way of determining this and for providing the type of professional development they need; it also makes what is provided to them more acceptable.

In many cases, the reason teachers do not accept the professional development that is provided to them is because they know there will be no continued support after it has been provided. In most situations, the school comes up with or gets sold on a cure-all program or model of doing something and presents it as professional development. Once the session is over, teachers go back to their classrooms with an idea of this plan and the school or district never mentions it again, nor do they offer additional training or support; however, they expect teachers to use what they learned from the training session in their classrooms.

When teachers experience something like this when nothing is ever mentioned about the training again (or there is no follow-up), then there is no acceptance from the teachers. It should also be noted, when teachers appear resistant to the professional development that was provided, school leaders should listen to them and why they feel the way they do about the professional development that was provided. Schools must stop doing things *to* teachers and start doing things *for* teachers.

CONCLUDING THOUGHTS

As this chapter has previously stated, for school instructional leaders, it is critical to find time during the school/workday to help teachers develop professionally. Teachers need to understand that time will be dedicated for that express purpose. It further must be understood that school-embedded professional development is an expectation and a great opportunity for teachers to discuss teaching and learning, and this should not be debatable.

If teachers and students in schools today are to flourish and excel in all they do, systemic change is necessary. There appears to be a lack of systematic evaluation efforts after professional development is offered. Even if the presentation was helpful, what good does it do if there is no plan in place to not only evaluate the training but also to evaluate the implementation and progress made after the training?

Teachers appear to want more opportunities to practice what they learn from professional development. As school leaders, some have found that facilitating these opportunities also creates opportunities to observe teacher progress and reinforce areas of weakness. It also provides additional opportunities and informal feedback regarding what types of follow-up training might need to be provided. Teachers present students with information several times, providing multiple opportunities for them to utilize that information; therefore, presenting information to teachers should not be any different.

For the most part, it appears teachers rarely view professional development as worth the time it requires them to spend outside of their classrooms. If schools would utilize their professional development budget wisely, it could be more beneficial to design professional development opportunities that incorporate the use of the skills and knowledge teachers possess. In any given school, there are teachers who possess numerous valuable skills and techniques. Schools should utilize these acquired skills as a source for providing professional development with each other.

Funds spent on professional development could be used for teachers creating opportunities to observe the desired skills and practices of other teachers within their building—or within their school district. This would allow teachers to implement and practice those learned skills within their classrooms. Instructional leaders could then observe the new practices, and it would allow them to identify gaps in learning and areas that may need improvement.

Once these gaps are identified, it will provide an opportunity to then bring to the school an outside professional development person in the particular area that needs to be addressed. This would also allow schools to differentiate the professional development based on teacher needs, and this would lead to greater acceptance from teachers. When differentiation of professional development is provided to teachers it will allow them to grow in specific areas of need and increase their capacity as teachers. When this is accomplished, the school will then become more functional and greater achievements can be seen in every classroom.

This differentiation in professional development is desperately needed and can truly assist instructional leaders and teachers in building the capacity that is desperately needed. At the same time working together in determining what teachers need in professional development builds capacity that can support the transformation of teaching and learning.

Quality embedded professional development in schools can assist in helping schools become more functional, but it should be focused on teacher capacity building and structured to support everything teachers do in the classroom. Providing this for teachers will help support everything the schools do, and without it, schools will see numerous challenges they will always be trying to overcome. This requires continuous evaluation, and there appears to be a lack of systematic evaluation efforts after most professional development is offered.

Even if the professional development that is provided is helpful, what good does it do if there is no plan in place to evaluate it relating to its effectiveness and how it supports what teachers do? To support the evaluation of professional development and to ensure continuous learning for teachers takes place, teachers need to be afforded the opportunity to provide feedback. Additionally, they need to be allowed to evaluate the professional development for its effectiveness, create opportunities for teachers to utilize the training they received with effective feedback, and be allowed to observe their peers, which facilitates more collaboration.[14]

Again, those who do practice this regularly find that by allowing teachers to provide feedback, this will lead to an increase in instructional skills that will directly impact student achievement.[15]

This chapter has attempted to explain that school-embedded professional development provided to teachers needs to improve drastically. School leaders must look closely at the professional development they are providing to make sure it will produce the intended results and, most importantly, provide continuous growth for teachers that can be transferred into the classroom.

NOTES

1. Thomas, L., & Beauchamp, C. (2011). Understanding new teachers' professional identities through metaphor. *Teaching and Teacher Education, 27,* 762–69. doi: 10.1016/jtquate. 2010.12.007.

2. Boyer, E. L. (1995). *The basic school: A community for learning.* San Francisco: Jossey-Bass.

3. The Mirage: Confronting the Hard Truth About Our Quest for Teacher Development. (2015). TNTP Reimagine Teaching, 1–68. Retrieved March 22, 2021 from https://tntp.org/assets/documents/TNTP-Mirage_2015.pdf.

4. Nussbaum-Beach, S. (2015, August 28). *Powerful learning source: 10 things teachers want in professional development.* Retrieved March 28, 2021 from https://plpnetwork.com/2015/08/28/10-teachers-professional-development/.

5. Darling-Hammond, L., Hyler, M. E., Gardner, M. (2017). *Effective Teacher Professional Development.* Palo Alto, CA: Learning Policy Institute.

6. Loucks-Horsley, S. (1995). Professional development and the learner centered school. *Theory into Practice: Creating learner centered schools, 34* (4), 265–71.

7. Kennedy, M. M. (1987, January). *Inexact sciences: Professional education and the development of expertise.* Retrieved April 10, 2021 from https://www.researchgate.net/publication/234762570_Inexact_Sciences_Professional_Education_and_the_Development_of_Expertise_Issue_Paper_87-2.

8. Strickland, C. (2009). *Professional development for differentiating instruction.* Alexandria, VA: ACSD Books.

9. Loucks-Horsley, S. (1995). Professional development and the learner centered school. *Theory into Practice: Creating learner centered schools, 34* (4), 265–71.

10. Rallis, S. F., & Goldring, E. B. (2000). *Principals of dynamic schools: Taking charge of change.* Thousand Oaks, CA: Corwin Press.

11. Perez, A. L. V., Milstein, M. M., Wood, C. J., & Jacquez, D. (1999). *How to turn a school around: What principals can do.* Thousand Oaks, CA: Corwin Press.

12. Sparks, D., & Hirsh, S. (2000, May 24). *Strengthen professional development.* Retrieved April 15, 2021 from https://www.edweek.org/leadership/opinion-strengthening-professional-development/2000/05.

13. Bill & Melinda Gates Foundation. (2014). *Teachers know best: Teachers' views on professional development.* Retrieved April 17, 2021 from http://www.usprogram.gatesfoundation.org/news-and-insights/articles/teachers-know-best-teachers-views-on-professional-development.

14. Jacob, A. C., & McGovern, K. (August 28, 2015). *The Mirage: Confronting the Hard Truth About Our Quest for Teacher Development.* Retrieved from https://tntp.org/assets/documents/TNTP-Mirage_2015.pdf.

15. Holloway, J. H. (Spring, 2006). *Connecting professional development to student learning gains.* Retrieved April 22, 2021 from https://www.https://files.eric.ed.gov/fulltext/EJ773253.pdf.

Chapter Seven

Movement and Learning in the Classroom

Over the last few decades, physical education and recess continue to steadily decline in schools across America. Simultaneously, there is an increase in the expectation for schools to encourage students to live a healthy and active lifestyle. It is therefore extremely important that school leaders understand this while working with teachers to help them in their work with students in their classrooms to live healthy lifestyles to support their learning.

Clearly, evidence provides support that students who are more active demonstrate sharpened focus, faster cognitive processing, and more successful memory retention than students who are less active.[1] This chapter relates specifically how educators can embed more active learning in the classroom, and how that can have a positive impact on learning and students' social and emotional skills.

It is obvious that research in this area indicates the numerous benefits of including physical activity in the classroom and how it can benefit student learning. Additionally, multiple forms of brain research and educational studies show that movement can play a critical role in student learning and retaining information; plus, it can also provide numerous other lifelong benefits. At the same time, common sense tells us that exercise is important.

Repeatedly, studies elaborate on students who are more active demonstrating sharpened focus, faster cognitive processing, and more successful memory retention than students who are less active. It is also noteworthy and should be understood by educators that when students exercise, the brain releases four key chemicals: serotonin, dopamine, endorphins, and cortisone. All of these can foster mental comprehensibility, which can improve learning along with improving physical and neurological health.[2]

It is equally important for school leaders and teachers to know and understand that allowing students to daily maintain physical activity for at least thirty to sixty minutes is known to reduce behavior and mental health issues and improve attention, which is believed to create more engaging, meaningful classes.[3] It is apparent that teachers are left with limited time to instruct students in reading and mathematical concepts while also giving critical areas, such as social studies and science, limited time for instruction.

It must be asked, With the demands that appear to be placed on teachers and school leaders, how can they find sufficient time to add physical movement instruction in their classrooms? It is understood that schools expect teachers to differentiate their instruction to meet the needs of those students who are falling below the standard learning expectations or have learning needs that must be addressed prior to learning.[4] At the same time, the instructional demands placed on teachers are coupled with a significant population of students who are identified with learning, behavioral, or other issues.

In addition, many states have mandated *blocks of minutes* that are around three hours—specifically, to address math and reading objectives. During this time, students are expected to sit and practice being quiet. With these demands, it is critical teachers utilize best educational and teaching practices and integrate subjects to increase opportunities for student learning; thus, physical movement instruction should be incorporated into lessons in every classroom.

With this in mind, ideas have evolved to include movement in the classroom, such as brain breaks, yoga, and action-based learning. Educators who work closely with students fully understand that exercise does help students with concentration, and, more specifically, it can decrease classroom management issues. At the same time, conversations with medical doctors provide evidence that exercise can help those students who are in states of depression, and it is obvious this is a problem with some students today.

The concept of action-based learning is increasingly becoming a focus in education across the country. Action-based learning is based on research concluding that students experience improved memory retention, increased focus and attention, improved grades, and less behavioral issues when the link between movement and learning is included in the classroom. School leaders and teachers should focus on this as they implement action-based learning in all facets of schooling.

Once it is implemented in schools, teachers may feel overwhelmed. But once they get involved in the process of implementation, they usually are totally convinced it is best for their students, and it can transform students' lives and their learning. There also are several claims that student behavioral issues decrease with the use of action-based learning labs. This is something all schools and parents should want. The ultimate focus is to use movement to enhance lessons that are already being taught during the school day—without needing extra materials, time, or money.

IMPACT OF PHYSICAL MOVEMENT ON THE BODY

In elementary schools, there appears to be noticeable interest in movement in the classroom through the viewpoint of things such as hands-on learning, project-based learning, and play. However, at the secondary level, this seems to not exist. Even with generous amounts of research encouraging movement as part of a strong educational program with multiple benefits (including increased student learning), these ideas have only been integrated into early and elementary classrooms.

Even more concerning is the fact that many of these ideas are often practices that become educational fads. School districts looking for the next big thing often push these practices on teachers; they do not offer appropriate ongoing training or have appropriate professional development time to focus on incorporating them into their lessons. This is a huge problem and causes many educators to become frustrated.

This is another example where school districts have no idea of the benefits that could be provided to their students through proper training and instruction relating to movement (that research strongly supports and has provided strong evidence as helpful and needed for student learning). Another attempt at helping more students succeed through movement is the failed attempt to improve student test scores. Too much focus is placed on this and, therefore, state testing becomes another attempt at placing limitations on movement and hands-on practices such as art, music, and physical education.

This is something that needs careful consideration by policy makers and educators, for it is a proven fact that movement and exercise do impact a person's well-being and mentality. It is imperative for instructional leaders and teachers to stop the trend of students' being required to remain stationary for long periods of time, with their only movement consisting of going from one classroom to another.

As this occurs, students are not being provided the opportunity to move to the point where they are able to maximize their learning potential. For those individuals who have been a pre-K–12 educator for any period of time, they know that students are not reaching their full academic potential because educators see that the average attention span of the vast majority of students is not very long. What is normally done when this occurs is that extended periods of time are devoted to classroom instruction.

These longer periods of time should be broken into smaller fragments of time, so students can experience movement that would also aid them and support better time dedicated to learning. Research involving movement and learning in the classroom clearly explains that fitness opportunities in schools lead to short- and long-term benefits, including better focus, retention, less absenteeism due to better health, and preventing long-term overall health issues including diabetes and obesity.[5]

Currently, the educational system promotes the idea of enabling students to become well-rounded individuals, with the focus on the whole child instead of the narrow perspective of focusing only on the mastery of academic content. Educators should promote and support student understanding of a healthy lifestyle; schools represent an ideal place to do this, but there again, are educators provided the necessary skills through professional development to support healthy living for their students?

Movement is effective in improving health through physical changes that occur when exercising. First, the process elevates the heart rate and oxygen consumption, stimulating the body and brain with oxygen and glucose, which improves overall health and mental focus. Multiple examples of research provide evidence that adding movement into instructional activities and transitions is part of the best practices to improve focus and retention in students' learning enhancing academic growth.

It is understood that educators are not certified to practice medicine; however, the research is there and does support movement as an activity that does promote better bodily functions that can promote greater efficiency for students and support better learning. The idea of movement integrated into classroom instruction through best practices creates active learning, leading to improved learning and better psychological outcomes for students.[6] It is vital for educators to understand the importance of this integration of brain-based and action-based learning while teaching because it allows teachers to better meet the totality of their students' needs.

Movement in the classroom comes from brain-based learning, which is based on the concept of using the brain, movement, visual, and auditory senses as a part of the learning process. This allows students to make new connections between content with previous ideas and new content to build upon prior knowledge. This should be what educators want to see from every student and, therefore, it is imperative that educators make every effort to incorporate these brain-based learning concepts into the education of all students.

HOW THE BRAIN WORKS IN STUDENTS

For teachers and school leaders to help students learn and understand the importance of movement as part of best practices (and to create active learning), there needs to be an understanding by educators about how children's and adolescents' brains work, relating to the processes associated with learning. This important learning for educators could very easily be provided in professional development school districts could provide teachers and school leaders.

This type of professional development is something that is needed, and teachers would support this because they would see how it would benefit students in their classrooms. It has been verified numerous times that during the later elementary years and early middle school years, the child's brain activity is mostly in the posterior regions where the areas for auditory, visual, and tactile functioning intersect.

This intersection is called the association area of the brain and generally contains information that has been learned and is now stored. This is the information that is commonly measured on achievement tests and verbal-based ability tests. Educators should be aware that cognitive learning and physical activity correlate, resulting in a positive trend of significant support for each other. Furthermore, *tactile*, or sense of touch and movement, learning and instructional practices can help improve a child's concentration and learning capacity, increasing self-confidence.[7]

It is vital that all educators understand this and can apply this to the child's learning environment. However, most educators are not aware of this information, because school districts have failed to provide appropriate professional development relating to this. Every educator should desire for all students to improve their concentration and learning capacity to support better self-confidence.

Multiple examples of research have concluded there is sufficient evidence to support that there are connections between the brain's performance and physical engagement. This research clearly suggests the brain lights up the same when a student is engaged in academic performance tasks, such as reading and mathematics, or physical activities, such as running. Therefore, physical movement in education is a gateway for increasing learning and memory along with mental health.

Also, this type of active learning provides students a way to maintain focus and learn complex concepts with better retention through movement. All educators must understand, when students are actively engaged in physical activity, there is a greater possibility that students will be more engaged in the learning process; therefore, creating optimal learning environments for all students through movement is extremely important.

EMBEDDING ACTION-BASED LEARNING IN SCHOOLS

Many schools have incorporated movement into their daily education of students, and one of the techniques used is through the use of action-based learning labs. Several schools have developed these labs that contain exercise equipment that enables students to exercise while learning, and it has been proven to support their physical and mental health. Action-based learning is used in ways that can improve learning through movement, and it is based on research that does support exercise and learning that can lead to greater depths of student achievement.

This is something all educators should desire and try to do as much possible: make exercise and learning become a reality in their schools. It is important to understand, with any exercise equipment there could be problems in how the equipment is used properly, and teachers should keep a watchful eye on their students while using the equipment. To maximize the experience and results of the action-based learning, teachers need to be thoroughly trained in brain development and the movement of each exercise station.

This training should include a variety of ways to modify each activity and how to use resources that are manageable for all students. This training can be accomplished through the school providing professional development that supports action-based learning, and the training can also assist teachers in understanding how to provide differentiated instruction that can significantly benefit the learning needs for every student.

When using and supporting action-based learning in the classroom and the various stations, teachers must realize that one station targets the body's vestibular system. This controls balance and spatial awareness, which strengthens students' ability to place words and letters on a page, for when a student walks or crawls in specific patterns, the brain's ability to encode symbols is increased.[8] If teachers are thoroughly educated on the movements and the correlation each movement has on learning, they can assign students to specifically work in a certain station with the right academic material to help a particular student make or build connections that may have been underdeveloped.

This is critical and supports the student's ability to learn. Overall, action-based learning labs have the potential to engage and promote learning while decreasing behavior issues, and these results can be maximized if slight changes are made to help teachers use stations specifically to address every student's needs. Again, if the school provides proper professional development for teachers in this area, it can greatly support what they are trying to do.

SCHOOL LEADERSHIP NEEDED FOR ACTION-BASED LEARNING TO BE SUCCESSFUL

For educators to recognize that action-based learning provides optimal learning environments for all students, there are some strategies school leaders can employ to start the journey and apply movement in the classroom. Educators who try to gain experience incorporating movement into the classroom encourage this by using a combination of strategies useful to improve instruction. To help teachers incorporate movement in their classroom, school leaders need to create planning time for teachers to work together with their grade partners.

When implementing action-based learning in the classroom, it is extremely helpful to teachers if they are allowed to use a common planning time. Using common planning times is very supportive for integrating action-based learning into the classroom as it allows teachers to work together, have ownership of their own personal growth, and develop trust in the process that enables them to take an instructional risk (that is often beneficial for student learning).

If there are no multiple teachers for each grade level, school leaders should allow teachers to work above and below their particular grade level. This allows teachers who are working together and who share a planning period to collaborate on lesson plans, discuss activities with clear objectives that include physical activities, and learn from each other, resulting in students achieving more.[9]

School leaders and teachers must know that integrating movement in the academic classroom can be accomplished in a variety of ways, from teachers using resources and programs already available to creating and implementing other unique strategies. Action-based learning represents a program that adds movement into education; in addition, there are *brain breaks/energizers* a teacher can use on a smartboard for students to follow.

Energizers are classroom-based physical activities that are designed to help teachers integrate physical activity with academic concepts. Energizers were first developed by a team from the Activity Promotion Laboratory at East Carolina University. Energizers have proven to be easy to implement because both teachers and students enjoy the activities, and they also help students stay on task—and all educators know that students staying on task is crucial.[10]

Teachers who have used energizers in their classrooms say they are easy to implement because both teachers and students enjoy the activities, and all educators know that students staying on task is crucial. Energizers and brain breaks are also useful in helping to rest and refresh the brain either through a calming, breathing brain break, some light yoga, or an energizer that allows students to hop as they count.

At the same time, energizers and brain breaks are beneficial mental breaks that can be flexibly added into any schedule in the middle of or between core lessons or to address a student's immediate needs.[11] Many teachers have found it to be beneficial because it has changed the way they arrange the classroom and sitting options for students. This affords the opportunity for students to take ownership of their own learning and incorporate movement into the classroom as they learn.

USING STABILITY BALLS IN THE CLASSROOM

All school leaders and teachers must recognize there is a need to focus on the whole child; therefore, the emotional needs of students must also be taken into consideration and be met. There is significant research on the positive impact when using a stability ball, especially regarding students who demonstrate inattention, hyperactivity, and defiant behaviors. Using stability balls in the classroom can also allow teachers to see significant and positive results. The introduction of movement into the classroom through the use of stability balls positively improves student's attention span, thus reducing disruptive behaviors.[12]

The best practice for introducing a stability ball into the classroom is to allow students to choose between using a regular desk chair while sitting or using a stability ball. Establishing clear expectations for the use of stability balls through mini lessons and explicit modeling can be accomplished by posting instructions with pictures on the wall. Teachers should also demonstrate the proper way to sit on the ball. Teachers should include the following expectations:

- Do not bounce too high.
- Sit with both feet on the floor.
- Do not draw or mark on the ball.

It is important to start by introducing a few stability balls of different sizes to students during the day and then slowly add more sizes after all students have had about two weeks to practice using them. If a student does not follow these expectations, he or she can lose the privilege of sitting on the stability ball for the remainder of the day, but he or she can be allowed to use the ball the next day.

It must be understood when planning on incorporating movement into the classroom, instructional school leaders and teachers must think about how to make the content interactive and part of the class routine. Next, the classroom expectations for what the movements will and will not look like in each classroom are critical to establish. First, set the procedures for how the movement is supposed to look, so students know what is expected of them. Most importantly, explain the purpose of each exercise and activity.

Educators should not feel they need to change their teaching style; however, they should feel supported and empowered to add some new strategies to their instruction. Teachers might decide to create an ongoing game that involves movement, and this can add support to what they are teaching and what students are learning. Using stability balls allows teachers to focus on the whole child and to place attention on the broader needs of students.

Beyond standing desks and stability balls, there is the process of using movement as part of the instructional focus. When planning on incorporating movement into the class activity, the teacher needs to think about how to make the content interactive and part of the class routine. Once the teacher has decided this, then it is critical the teacher make sure their students understand what the movement will be. Teachers should first set the procedures of what the movement is supposed to look like, so students know what is expected of them.

For example, if the teacher is teaching about syllables, they can post various words all over the classroom with different numbers of syllables. This allows teachers to better meet the needs of their students by allowing students to do more complex words while still meeting the needs of those who need simple, one-syllable words. This is a great way to differentiate instruction because it allows teachers to learn more, and it can also maximize the teacher's belief that every student can and has the ability to learn.[13]

Differentiated instruction also provides multiple ways to respond to diverse learners' needs, including those who are English Language Learners. This is a challenge in many schools today; these students appear to struggle, and educators must do all they can to support and provide for their learnings needs.

For example, English Language Learners need environments where instructional practice integrates understanding group practices as well as individual student variations. Overall, there is a need to be able to differentiate instruction for the individual while allowing time for collaboration to enhance learning for English Language Learners—which is increasingly plausible with movement in the classroom. It is apparent, the more students are involved in the learning process, the more they retain and the more meaningful the learning becomes. That can create a new quality of learning for students.

School leaders and teachers must find ways to make their instruction more active. For example, the entire class can create a foldable about syllables and encourage movement in the classroom as students are doing the folding. Teachers can then have the students (when they feel ready) walk around the room to help each other or ask questions from one another. When the foldable is complete, the teacher can then make the material interactive as part of the procedure by playing music as students walk around the room and practice reading the words.

If students need help, they can ask for help sounding out words together. They should not be allowed to stop and start writing. They must move the entire time the music is playing. When the music stops, they go to a word (with no more than two students at a word at any time). Students can then write the word and move again when the music starts. This allows for a pre-assessment of the student's background knowledge.

This also provides a safe climate for learning as students who need more time will not feel like they stand out for taking too long to complete the activity. If a student needs more time, they can finish writing while other students are moving. Students can go to words they understand, as this allows teachers to assess their knowledge. At the same time, students can write words under the number of syllables, which allows teachers to assess the students' abilities with the target skill.

This procedure takes some practice for students to understand how to move as they should not run or talk loudly, etc. If the weather does not allow outside play time, teachers can change the movements to meet the energy level of their students. When this does happen, teachers may have their students stomp like a dinosaur, hop like a frog, do lunges, or other forms of movement. Each time the students move, they can represent different forms of movement. This activity can take as little as five minutes, yet be a routine part of the day that reoccurs.

If teachers decide to make this an ongoing part of instruction, this activity allows students to monitor their own learning. While doing this in the classroom, students may have words written under the wrong number. However, as they learn and interact with the syllables, even the movement of saluting their throat as they sound out words can change their previous thinking. The best practice would be to engage students in this activity at least once a day. The majority of the words should stay up with a few changes weekly, as the formative assessment reveals students' gains of knowledge.

This type of classroom instruction can integrate multiple subjects at one time, including science and social studies concepts or spelling and vocabulary words. When these procedures are routinely practiced and the material is consistently covered, this activity becomes a continuous review to ensure students are not forgetting concepts. At the same time, these activities provide consistent opportunities for students who are still struggling with this concept to understand the objective. Additionally, this activity is a great extension for early finishers.

It is also a great activity for students who finish early, as they can grab their foldable and walk around the room and add words to their foldable.

Therefore, active-learning strategies need to be teacher friendly, time efficient, and, most importantly, make learning fun for students with the educational goal of helping students release stress, learn concepts, and self-regulate themselves. This also allows teachers to take an objective or worksheet and make it come alive.

Another example of making worksheets come alive to help students learn literature standards is to put passages up from a story all over the room. While music is playing, students can dance around the room with a partner until the music stops. After this, students would share their ideas with other groups while learning the language of debate, the art of asking clarifying questions, giving and receiving constructive criticism, and working collaboratively, along with self-reflection and changing of their thinking.

When this form of action-based learning is combined with collaborative learning, students receive the benefits of physical movement. Doing this allows students to take responsibility for working together, building knowledge together, and changing and evolving together. While this is taking place it also supports teachers and allows them to adapt their teaching style to better meet students' learning needs.[14] Additionally, each group of students may work on the same concepts, or different groups can work on different objectives depending on the students' needs. This, again, allows for differentiated instruction.

For these reasons, action-based learning is a powerful method for educators to use to engage student interest and to modify tasks that can meet each student's ability. It has been theorized that educators should create purposeful instruction by considering the differences among students' background knowledge, acknowledging each student's strengths while accommodating their limitations through activities, and considering their substantial experiences, allowing the students to attain their zone of proximal development.[15]

CONCLUDING THOUGHTS

It may be tricky to measure the specific impact of action-based learning labs (although they may offer many benefits). Additionally, there are some constraints to maximizing their benefits because of limited time, equipment, and training. Therefore, those school leaders and teachers who are interested in adding active learning should consider starting changes slowly by integrating standing desks or balance balls to the classroom.

Also, teachers can include active learning in their instruction by using collaboration and movement through energizers or ongoing activities that are part of the academic process. It is important to include research that expresses the need for action-based learning, meaningful feedback, and collaborative opportunities—all to be used together to maximize student emotional and academic growth and learning.

Those teachers who think critically and are engaged in activity-based learning provide opportunities for collaborative discussion and experiences for their students, and they are provided meaningful feedback that allows students to take responsibility for their learning. This is something that is needed in schools today. Action-based learning integrates learning theory, by which all educators should understand that learning is a developmental process where information is built on prior knowledge students have learned.

As students walk around the room and adjust their learning, they are working within their zone of proximal development, which requires a collaborative relationship between teacher and student.[16] In addition, action-based learning combined with collaborative opportunities create an environment where the learning develops into a social context, encouraging the development of cognitive and communication skills. Movement in the classroom provides optimal opportunities for educators to utilize as few as five minutes to get students moving and working collaboratively in a social context.

Research clearly supports the claim that tells educators there are various benefits of increasing physical activity levels and improving the personal fitness of children/adolescents. Some of the benefits of active learning are increased blood and oxygen flow (which positively affects physical health), mental well-being, and cognitive development, which all contribute to better academic achievement.[17] At the same time, the positive increase in student attention spans, memory, and emotional health is significant when active learning is part of the best instructional practices, and teachers can clearly observe these things in their students.

Most importantly, this provides teachers with meaningful feedback that is quick, focused on what the students did well, and sets a goal for them to focus on where they can apply more effort for their improvement. Constantly, when trying to improve student feedback, teachers can rely on a powerful quote that says, "Feedback is a gift and ideas are the currency for further success."[18]

Students need to see teachers value their feedback, as it will inspire them to move to greater depths in their learning and understanding. Students and educators working together within this mindset can make feedback a normal process that takes place in the classroom. When this happens in the classroom, it also allows students to be more engaged in their own learning that can assist them with their specific academic needs.

Finally, school leaders, teachers, and students play a vital and active role in the successful implementation of active learning. A plethora of research indicates students, teachers, and school leaders, along with other stakeholders, enjoy the benefits of active learning through students being engaged. It also fosters fewer student referrals and higher academic gains. Teachers and school leaders should learn how to use and embed various physical activities in the teaching process.

Establishing options for students to choose from, such as being active when sitting or standing, allows them to be self-reflective and provides an opportunity for students to discover their own learning style needs. This is critical for them to become successful learners. This addition to teaching can greatly enhance greater depths of student achievement, and this is something all educators should want to take place in classrooms.

NOTES

1. Dooley, M. (2008). *Telecollaborative language learning: A guidebook to moderating intercultural collaboration online.* Peter Lang AG, Internationaler Verlag der Wissenschaften.

2. Biller, L. (2003). *Creating brain friendly classrooms: Practical instructional strategies for educators.* New York, NY: Rowman & Littlefield.

3. Strong, W. B., Malina, R. M., Blimkie, C. J., Daniels, S. R., Dishman, R. K., Gutin, B., & Rowland, T. (2005). Evidence based physical activity for school-age youth. *The Journal of Pediatrics, 146,* 732–37.

4. Tomlinson, C. A., & McTighe, J. (2006). *Integrating differentiated instruction & understanding by design: Connecting content and kids.* Alexandria: ASCD.

5. Trudeau, F., & Shepherd, R. J. (2005, February 28). *Physical education, school physical activity, school sports and academic performance.* Retrieved December 23, 2021 from https://ijbnpa.biomedcentral.com/track/pdf/10.1186/1479-5868-5-10.pdf.

6. Chisholm, A., & Spencer, B. (2017, March). *Let's get moving: Eight ways to teach information literacy using kinesthetic activities.* Retrieved January 3, 2021 from University of Pittsburgh, Website: http://palrap.org/ojs/index.php/palrap/article/view/141.

7. Tomporowski, P. D., McCullick, B. A., & Pesce, C. (2015). *Enhancing children's cognition with physical activity games.* Champaign, IL: Human Kinetics Publishers.

8. Mitchell, D. (2012). *Learning through movement and music.* Champaign, IL: Human Kinetics Publishers.

9. Villa, R. A., & Nevin, A. (2006). The many faces of collaborative planning and teaching. *Theory into Practice, 23* (3), 34–41.

10. Mahar, M., Kenny, R., Shields, T., Scales, D., & Collins, G. (2006). *Energizers: Classroom-based physical activities K-12.* Retrieved November 18, 2021 from East Carolina University, Website: https://thescholarship.ecu.edu/handle/10342/5943?show=full.

11. Mahar, M. (2011, June). *Impact of short bouts of physical activity on attention-to-task in elementary school children.* Retrieved November 18, 2021 from http://www.researchgate.netpublication/49798764_Impact_of

_short_bouts_of_physicalactivity_on_attention-to-task_in_elementary_school_children.

12. Gaston, A., Moore, S., & Butler, L. (2016). Sitting on a stability ball improves attention span and reduces anxious/depressive symptomatology among grade 2 students: A prospective case-control field experiment. *International Journal of Educational Research, 77,* 136–42.

13. Tomlinson, C. A., & McTighe, J. (2006). *Integrating differentiated instruction & understanding by design: Connecting content and kids.* Alexandria: ASCD.

14. Lane S. (2016). Promoting collaborative learning among students. *American Journal of Educational Research, 4* (8), 602–607.

15. Vygotsky, L. (1978). Interaction between learning and development. *Readings on the development of children, 23* (3), 34–41.

16. Ibid.

17. Grissom, J. B. (2005). Physical fitness and academic achievement. *Journal of Exercise Physiology Online, 8* (1).

18. Trinka, J., & Wallace, L. (2020, December 2). *The importance of feedback.* Retrieved December 23, 2021 from https://medium.com/age-of-awareness/the-importance-of-feedback-28e8e8d31d1e.

About the Authors

Dr. John R. Jones is a clinical professor in instructional leadership at the University of Oklahoma. He currently serves as the program coordinator for the Educational Leadership Program in the Jeannine Rainbolt College of Education. Beginning with the academic year of 2022, he will be starting his fifty-first year in education. For sixteen of those years, he served as a public schoolteacher and a high school principal in three different school districts.

In 1986 he transitioned into higher education, which has allowed him to serve at four different universities in three states. His leadership experience is very extensive, as ten of those years he served as a university vice president, five years as a graduate dean, and eight years as a dean of a college of education. In 2015 he started working for the second time for the University of Oklahoma. His experiences in public school and in higher education have given him a rich background that allows him to see things through multiple lenses.

One of the things readers will learn from this book is that great leadership is an art and is something that is needed today more than ever in our schools. Regarding this, his leadership and teaching experiences have afforded him the expertise needed to publish numerous articles that relate specifically to instructional leadership and what instructional leaders should do as they work with teachers to enhance and improve the quality of instruction.

Misty Henry has taught for many years and, currently, she is an instructional coach for Oklahoma City Public Schools. She is a teacher scholar and is currently completing her PhD in educational leadership at the University of Oklahoma. She has won numerous awards as a teacher of excellence; most recently, she was recognized by television station KFOR in Oklahoma City as part of their Thankful for Teacher Awards. She was one of ten teachers in the state of Oklahoma who won the award. She has written and published numerous articles on teacher and student performance as well as lectured on, conducted, and published research on teacher excellence and instructional leadership.

www.ingramcontent.com/pod-product-compliance
Lightning Source LLC
Chambersburg PA
CBHW032216230426
43672CB00011B/2576